LUXURY LISTING SPECIALIST
DOMINATE LUXURY LISTINGS IN YOUR MARKET

Michael A. LaFido

The real estate industry has been doing the same things over and over again when it comes to selling luxury homes. In most marketplaces today the high-end luxury homes are not selling because the vast majority of agents rely solely on traditional marketing approaches taught by their brokers or real estate school. This practice personifies the definition of insanity: doing the same thing repeatedly and expecting different results.

If you commit to reading this book and take it very seriously, not only will you be able to attract more high-end clients, but more importantly you will be able to sell more luxury homes faster while netting the sellers more money.

It's time to raise the standards and take matters into your own hands.

MarketingLuxuryGroup.com

DEDICATION

This book is dedicated to all those luxury agents and brokers who are fed up with the "traditional" way of marketing luxury homes. (Or, I should say, traditional way of not marketing luxury houses.) Perhaps you are part of a big national brokerage or an office that specializes in luxury real estate. You might have expected the company owner to provide you with cutting-edge marketing tools, but instead all you have received are the same old trainings and collateral that everyone else uses.

If this sounds familiar, then this book is for you. It's time to take control of your business. After all, it's your business and it's your hard-earned reputation on the line. This book will show you how to dominate luxury listings in your market by attracting the right clients and getting their homes sold.

"We don't list homes, we market them. There is a calculated difference. We create massive exposure to get buyers, realtors, the community, and the press talking about the homes we market."

~ Michael LaFido

MarketingLuxuryGroup.com

ENDORSEMENTS FROM
INDUSTRY LEADERS

"Michael LaFido has developed a blueprint for success that gives both realtors and broker owners a turnkey system to dominate listing and selling luxury homes in ANY market."

> **- Chad Roffers,**
> **Chairman & Managing Director**
> **of Concierge Auctions**

"After attending Michael's all day seminar in Lewisville, Texas, I can at-test that agents who want to break into the luxury market, and/or are looking for very unique and aggressive marketing strategies to mar-ket for their luxury listings, this designation is a must. As agents there are many courses to choose from, but not all of them have substance! Michael is in the trenches and practices what he preaches."

> **- Olivier Mevellec,**
> **Co-founder & President of**
> **Global Marketing Agent**

"If you want to market high-end properties then Michael's Luxury course is a must. He is the expert, and he leads by example with his impressive portfolio of $1 million+ listings and sales. Michael recently gave a Marketing Luxury all day seminar to 122 of my agents in Dallas. They were more than impressed and virtually all of them are going for the LUXE designation offered by Michael. But even more important is the integrity and caliber of professionalism that Michael exudes. A real class act."

> **- Mark Wolfe,**
> **Owner of RE/MAX DFW Associates**

"Wow, I have never seen a more impressive approach to listing and marketing multi-million dollar properties. His inventory of homes reads like a Who's Who list of American's Best Real Estate Properties. I cannot imagine ANY seller, with a multi-million dollar property not listing with Mike. If you want to break into the multi-million dollar property market, or learn how to get your luxury listing sold, Michael is the person to talk to."

> - Judy LaDeur,
>   Founder and President of
>   The Profitable Recruiter and
>   Judy LaDeur International

"If you're ready to be more successful and reach a higher level, then read Mike's book. He has a true passion for making a positive difference!"

> - James Malinchak,
>   Featured on ABC's Hit TV Show,
>   *Secret Millionaire*
>   Author of the Top-Selling Book,
>   *Millionaire Success Secrets*
>   Founder, www.MillionaireFreeBook.com

ENDORSEMENTS FROM AGENTS ——

Here's what agents who attended one of
Michael's trainings had to say...

SUSAN D'AMICO
1st year in the business
**The reason I attended Michael's Luxury Training instead of a different one
was because:**
*"I'd rather start at the top and develop a stellar skill set and not waste my time
and money working my way to the middle (or last)"*

KIM HENLEY
$2M Producer
**Before this event the number one concern or worry
I had about selling luxury homes was:**
*"Not having confidence and wanting more experience
so that I feel more knowledgeable in luxury homes"*

TERRY HENDRICKS
$2M Producer
**The reason I attended Michael's Luxury Training
instead of a different one was because:**
"To gain a competitive edge over my competition"

SHERI STEVENSON
$8.5M Producer
**The reason I attended Michael's Luxury Training
instead of a different one was because:**
*"I want to work fewer units per year and make more
money with fewer work hours"*

SUSAN LUCKY SMITH

$9M Producer

The reason I attended Michael's Luxury Training instead of a different one was because:

"I would like to raise my average sales price"

IRYNA MITCHELL

$7M Producer

The reason I attended Michael's Luxury Training instead of a different one was because:

"I want to learn more about the luxury market from an actual professional who does it, not just some luxury real estate instructor"

NAMRATA BHATT

$10+ Million Producer

Additional Comments:

"Love it! Everyone who's in real estate MUST attend Michael's training!"

DEBBI McCOY

$12M Producer

This event was different than the trainings I have used in the past (or have heard about) because:

"Showed real life examples, in the trenches, hands on experience, honest and not 'classroom' training."

DAVID EUDY
$20M Producer

Before Michael's Luxury Training the number one concern or worry I had about selling luxury homes was:

"The time it takes to move luxury homes"

KIMBERLY BARTON
$30M Producer

Before Michael's Luxury Training the number one concern or worry I had about selling luxury homes was:

"Not having done an over $1 million-dollar sale before"

DONNA BRADSHAW
$35M Producer

Michael LaFido was different than the trainings I have seen in the past (or have heard about) because:
"The speaker has walked the walk"

VICTOR VO
$40M Producer

If I had a friend or family member that was a real estate agent in another city, I'd recommend LUXE to them primarily because:
"It's real. It's worked! Great visuals! Learn from the one who is doing it!"

Cyndy Caldwell Silva
Active 5 minutes ago

5:13 PM

Hi Michael, I just had to write you to tell you I just went to a seminar to hear the #1 KW Agent in the World, ███████ speak. Your seminar was soooo much better, I came home with a book of notes after listening to you speak, I came home with 2 pages of notes from ███. When I left your seminar I was so motivated and couldn't wait to implement your ideas. The best thing I got from ███ was handing out goodie bags at Open House, lol. So in a nutshell I just wanted to say YOU ROCK!!! Take Care, Cyndy Silva ☺

Thank you so much for the kind

Write a message...

ABOUT THE AUTHOR

Michael LaFido

Michael LaFido is a speaker, trainer, author, founder of the Marketing Luxury Group and creator of the Luxury Listing Specialist certification (LUXE). As a top producing, luxury real estate agent with over 17 years of experience in the Chicago market, Michael and his team have a wealth of knowledge to share. They have developed a method that takes a more comprehensive, proactive approach to marketing a home—a method now available to agents around the world.

Michael and his team assist other real estate agents and affluent home owners by providing premium bespoke services including "lifestyle marketing," consulting, and PR services to help agents and owners sell their luxury homes using proven and reputable strategies.

While many Realtors struggle to break into the luxury niche, it was relatively easy for LaFido once he introduced potential clients to fresh strategies like event-based marketing and videos featuring professional actors. This natural marketer readily admits to looking outside the real estate industry for ideas, transforming proven concepts into methods that have modernized luxury realty.

Michael also created the nationally recognized luxury certification for real estate agents that is known as the Luxury Listing Specialist Certification (LUXE). This new certification establishes a minimum set of standards for agents that represent luxury homes. While many Realtors struggle to break into the luxury niche, it was relatively easy for LaFido once he introduced potential clients to fresh strategies like event-based marketing and videos featuring professional actors. This natural marketer readily admits to looking outside the real estate industry for ideas, transforming proven concepts into methods that have modernized luxury realty. Many agents in the industry are calling Michael's methods "The New Standard" for marketing luxury homes today.

DISCLAIMER

This book was created for real estate agents either considering breaking into selling luxury homes or agents that specialize in selling luxury homes. This book is perfect for real estate agents who are looking for new approaches, innovative marketing, and proven repeatable strategies that work to sell real estate for top dollar. Armed with this information, agents reading this book will have the advantage in their marketplace and access to the proprietary systems and marketing to make them the leading real estate agent in their market. This book is not conventional by any means, but it has numerous proven strategies that have been successful time and time again. These strategies have been tested in many marketplaces at various price points. (It would be a huge mistake for you to think "this won't work in my market" because your market is different or your clients are different. Your market or clientele are not different.) These turnkey systems are not conventional and that is one of the reasons why our systems are so successful. This book will dive into the problems in the real estate industry today and also into different philosophies and strategies, outlining the pros and cons of each. At the end of this book, agents will be well informed and realize that there are better options to utilize than the traditional real estate marketing models.

This book will not be helpful for agents seeking the same strategies that most luxury real estate firms and "gurus" typically suggest. We won't be talking about those "traditional" marketing strategies because they simply don't work.

> **"One of the most important responsibilities real estate agents have is to make the home standout versus the competition to both buyers and agents. Unfortunately most agents fail miserably at this."**
> ~ Michael LaFido

MarketingLuxuryGroup.com

ACKNOWLEDGMENTS

Thank You!

This book would not be possible without the loving support of my wife, Amy. Countless numbers of long hours, late nights, and early mornings went into developing my real estate consulting businesses and creating this book. Thank you, Amy. I love you more than words can say. I would also like to thank my mother who has always believed in me and pushed me to "Keep Soaring" to new heights.

I'd also like to thank my football coaches at Wheaton South High School and Northern Michigan University. The life lessons I have learned from athletics has carried over to the real world.

Finally, thanks to my competition. You help keep that burning desire of mine "on" all the time.

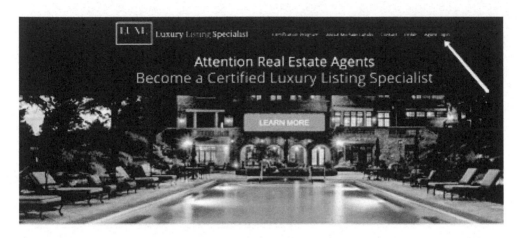

To help agents demonstrate their skills, I have created a luxury broker certification. This new designation establishes a minimum set of standards for agents. My program instills the same principles I outline in my book, "Marketing Luxury," and teach through my Marketing Luxury Group.

It offers potential clients third-party validation through documented, hands-on training and certification. Most agents spend years trying to secure luxury listings; many never get them. With this certification, agents have access to proven and repeatable marketing systems, which can be utilized in the marketing of their luxury listings. This certification and the training agents receive as part of this program will almost single-handedly pull the luxury real estate niche out of the Dinasauric Age. Agents are seeing astounding results from these pioneering methods.

To learn more on how to get certified, please visit
LuxuryListingSpecialist.com

ONLINE ACCESS TO ALL TRAINING AND MATERIALS

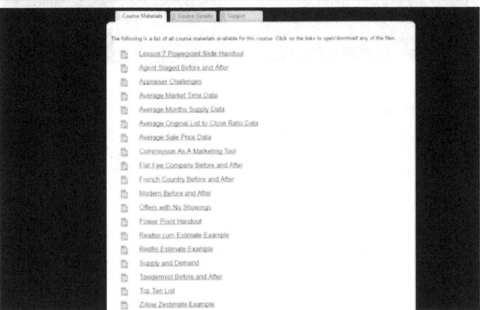

To learn more on how to get certified, please visit

LUXURYLISTINGSPECIALIST.COM

Want to break into selling high end homes? Subscribe to the Luxury Listing Specialist Podcast

MANAGEMENT & MARKETING

Where top luxury agents reveal their best practices PLUS interviews with real estate industry influencers, thought leaders and luxury marketing experts, you'll come away from each episode with new strategies and tactics to list and sell high-end homes in ANY market.

www.LuxuryListingPodcast.com

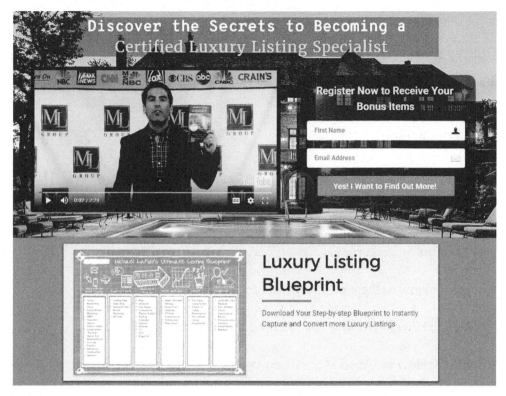

This bonus session includes Step-by-step video training on building a foundation to consistently sell luxury homes, the blueprint to attract luxury sellers, and how to use video to position yourself as a luxury authority in your market.

Get it NOW at
LUXURYLISTINGBLUEPRINT.COM

TABLE of CONTENTS

INTRODUCTION

This book is perfect for you if you want more high-end listings, buyers, and of course, luxury listings. This book was intended to be an easy read. It's a breath of fresh air that is desperately needed today in luxury real estate. Included in this book are a lot of pictures and quotes to help you understand crucial concepts and ideas. Want to differentiate yourself from your competition? Then this book is perfect for you whether you're in a buyer's market or a seller's market, and even if you have a saturated market of higher end homes currently on the market. Finally, if you're open to new marketing strategies, you're reading the right book. This book is an easy read that will give you insight on all markets and get you in the direction of selling more luxury homes.

WHAT THIS BOOK IS AND ISN'T

This book is not a bunch of theories. It isn't fluff from some former agent that doesn't practice what they preach. This book wasn't written by an agent who is in a marketplace where the average sale price is $1 million or more. There are a lot of so-called experts in real estate today who don't practice what they preach. It's easy to call yourself a luxury agent if you work in Beverly Hills or New York City because the price point lends itself to that business, but elsewhere, agents need effective strategies to help sell million-dollar homes.

The systems outlined in this book will work in any marketplace, for any price home and any style home. None of it works all the time, but all of it works the majority of the time, especially when the agent keeps practicing and building confidence. Keep an open mind. I guarantee you'll be better off after reading this book than you were before because you'll be armed with the tools you need to grow your business. You will be confident with the knowledge this book provides you, and I am certain that my advice will help you realize that making your mark in the high-end and luxury markets is within your reach.

How can you double your income this year? There are three easy ways to do it! The first is sell more homes. You might equate that with more work, but that's not necessarily the case. You can sell more homes without increasing your workload by maximizing your efficiency. By changing a few of your strategies and using the knowledge you learn in this book, you will earn more listing opportunities and connect with more buyers simply because you're working smarter.

You need to increase your conversion, which does not necessarily require working more leads, but it will increase your opportunities. Selling more homes requires new clients or more repeat business.

The second is to earn more profit per transaction. You can increase what you charge or you can just make more profit per transaction by cutting back on some "fat" like wasting marketing dollars. To increase what you charge means negotiating a higher commission. To sell high-end homes, most agents compete by lowering their fee. I'm charging my sellers a premium in my marketplace because they see the value of my work. It doesn't matter what you charge sellers; what matters is what they net, what they walk away with. Again, many agents discount their services, but I'm going to help you protect your fee. That's the fastest way for you to get a return on your investment for this course. Don't compete by lowering your fee. Eventually you're going to build up your confidence and your reputation, so you can justify increasing what you charge.

The third and probably the most effective way to double your income is to increase your average sale price. If the average sale price in your market is $150,000 and you increase it this year to $300,000, guess what? You've just doubled your income selling the same quantity of homes.

CHAPTER 1 | How to Define Luxury Real Estate in Most Markets

"I can't understand why people are frightened of new ideas. I'm frightened of the old ones."
- John Cage

It is difficult to break into the luxury real estate market because most luxury sellers rarely give you the opportunity to meet with them until you can show them that you have successfully sold similar homes in that area. You have to build their trust. If you're just starting, my advice is to do anything possible to list or sell your first high-end or luxury home. Once you make the first couple of sales it's easier to sustain business with those clients.

I have clients across the world, and I can tell you the upper-end market is definitely a buyer's market with a lot of inventory out there. It's going to take an agent who's aggressive and thinks outside the box while using cutting-edge strategies to get showings and to get these homes sold.

Luxury is constantly redefined in real estate, just as new sports cars and fashions appear and change the market. So how do we define luxury real estate? Some people classify by the style of the house, or perhaps the finishes and the product brands in the home. I know different brokerages and different real estate firms define luxury real estate differently, but for this book we're going to define luxury as a home that is three times more than the market average sale price. If the market sale price average is $150k, we're going to define luxury at $450k and above. If the market average sale price is $500k, then we're going to define luxury real estate at $1.5 million.

Every marketplace has luxury homes; however, when people think luxury, they think McMansions or estate homes, and that's not always the case. When I talk about high-end and luxury, there is a difference. I define high-end as two times the average market sale price while luxury is three times the market average. There really isn't a huge difference in high-end and luxury in terms of the homes themselves, but most marketplaces do have more high-end homes than luxury, so that's why we use both terms.

To take action, you need to develop graphs and other visuals that can articulate data for luxury and high-end real estate for your marketplace as well as globally. Are you in a buyer's market or a seller's market? High-end and luxury homes start at what price point for your market? You need to know this information. You need to align yourself with luxury affiliates and become a student of local and global luxury trends. Every ambitious agent in this business wants to break into the luxury market, so you need to set yourself apart by proving you have excellent market knowledge and proven plans to successfully help homeowners sell their homes.

This Book Is Perfect If You:

- Want More Higher End Listings & Buyers
- Want To Differentiate Yourself From Your Competition
- Are In A Buyer's Market
- Are In A Seller's Market
- Have A <u>Saturated</u> Market Of Higher End Homes Currently On The Market
- Are Open To New <u>Marketing</u> Strategies

Double Your Income

3 Ways To Earn More Money This Year:

1. Sell More Homes
   -Requires More Leads/Opportunities
   -New Clients & Repeat Business
2. Increase What You Charge
   -Profit Per Transaction
3. Increase Your **<u>Average Sale Price</u>**

Attract vs Chase!

Analytics For Your Area

Higher End Pricing Starts At $_____?

Luxury Pricing Starts At $_____?

Buyer's Market or Seller's Market?

Average Days On Market?

List Price To Sale Price Ratio?

Other Factors?

> **"We don't just list homes—we market them. There's a calculated difference."**
>
> **- Michael LaFido**

**LUXURY
LISTING
SPECIALIST
PODCAST**

CHAPTER 2 | How to Double Your Income While Working Less

"Don't think like a real estate agent, think like a marketer."

- Michael LaFido

Real estate is a show and tell industry, just like back in kindergarten. The teacher would have you bring a prop or a toy from home and you got to share stories and information with your classmates. I remember those days fondly, and now my wife and I get to share those experiences as parents. My middle child's name is Vince. "Vinnie the bulldozer" as we call him. He's getting older now, but when he was younger, he had show and tell and he was supposed to bring something in to his class that started with the letter M. Now you'll notice in the picture to the bottom Vince is holding a Moscow Mule mug. A Moscow Mule is an adult beverage that has liquor in it and is served in a copper mug, which is kind of a signature cocktail. To our surprise, one day he brought home my Moscow Mule mug in his backpack.

Amy said, "Vince, why was this is your backpack?" He said, "Well it was show and tell and we were supposed to bring something in that started with the letter M, and I brought in a Moscow Mule mug because it started with three M's." Thankfully, his teacher, Miss Carson, had a good sense of humor because otherwise we might have been in the principal's office the next day. Real estate is a show and tell industry because you have to be a good presenter—organized, engaging, knowledgeable about your topic. Like the Moscow Mule mug example, it's always good to keep your sense of humor as well, because real estate is full of surprises.

It's very important for you as an agent that you know your numbers in your local marketplace. You need to know the analytics for your area. You need to know price points for high-end homes in your area, plus luxury numbers too. You need to know whether it is a buyer's market or a seller's market for each of those categories because you might have a seller who is misinformed based on the experiences or advice his or her friends have shared, especially those who have sold lower-priced homes.

In this chapter, we're going to be talking about the "inner game," better known as your mindset. Again, the inner game is so important and I can't stress that enough. Conquering your inner game will help you have your best year ever and double your income. There are a lot of misconceptions about selling luxury homes or getting into luxury real estate as an agent. I call them limiting beliefs. You do not have to be a top producer or veteran agent before you can start selling high-end homes. You do not need to be wealthy. You do not need to live in a large home. You do not need to drive an expensive car. You do not need to work in a certain office. These are some of the big misconceptions that people believe an agent needs to have in order to sell real estate. That is simply not true. You do not need to have a huge home, be with a certain brokerage, be wealthy, or work in the industry for X number of years before you can dive into selling high-end or luxury homes. Those are all limiting beliefs. Don't let

those misconceptions hold you back.

I am going to share with you how you can make more money without making more cold calls, knocking on more doors, or buying cold, recycled Internet leads like everybody else. You will not be sitting in more open houses or spending more money on postcards and mailers. There is an easier solution for getting ahead by positioning yourself as the industry expert. You can actually attract high-net-worth clients versus chasing them. We have talked about doubling your income, but it's not all about money, folks. I assure you it's not just about money. I can tell you that money provides freedom, freedom equals time for family, friends, and activities you enjoy. If you make more money you can hire more assistants, so you can take more time off to spend however you want. If you take more time off you have time to build stronger relationships and a chance to pursue the things that make you happy. I continue to remember these points after learning them from my speaking coach, James Malinchak.

Now I want to go over three steps in designing your luxury business. These are the core foundational principles. Number one, you need to know what you want. You need to be specific. If we were to meet three years from today, what would have happened in those three years from both a personal and a professional standpoint for you to be happy about your progress? That is how you set goals. Think about what you're doing today. Is it leading toward those goals? If the answer is no, then we have to take a look at it.

Number two, why do you want it? Again, why do you want it, what is "it"? When you're setting goals, you've got to know why you want success. Be specific. Number three is you have to create your plan. You've just got to do it to succeed. What needs to change for you to double your income this year? Is it your mindset? Is it your inner game? Is it improving your systems? Maybe they're not working. Look objectively at

your conversion, or perhaps your marketing. Don't reinvent the wheel. Tony Robbins once said, "Success leaves clues." Model someone else that has been there and learn from his successes and failures. I know I have gained a lot from studying what has worked versus what hasn't in my business. I've invested hundreds of thousands of dollars in my career for coaches and gurus, models and systems. I've taken what's worked and what hasn't, and I put it all together. That's what I'm sharing with this book that you are reading. Remember this statement by Tony Robbins, "Success leaves clues."

Have you ever heard of Darren Hardy? He wrote a great book called *The Compound Effect.* His advice is to do fewer things, do them more often, and get better at them. Many agents have "shiny object syndrome." They get distracted by new tactics or products. However, when you have too many different aspects of your business to focus on, it creates confusion and lack of focus. You will be more successful if you work to perfect one strategy and hone in on the strengths you have.

You need to know what your time is worth for you to prioritize what's important. Again, focus on fewer things, practice them more often, and work to get better at them. Let's talk about some habits of successful entrepreneurs and high-net-worth individuals. They network and prospect daily, and their results speak volumes. Don't be shy. You have to sell yourself. Don't look at it as bragging. This is your opportunity to share your successes with potential clients so they see your value. When you have a successful sale, post it on social media. Ask for client testimonials because it's more effective when somebody else talks about a great experience working with you. Generate leads via public speaking. Build long-term client relationships. Strengthen your personal brand by being active in your community. Develop a social media and online presence with the look and feel that's congruent with your message. These are all effective strategies that allow new and potential clients to get to know

you and build trust in your brand.

Another idea is to cultivate media contacts. I will be talking about press and public relations in Chapter 12. Work to develop relationships with other successful agents and people that deal with high-net-worth individuals such as bankers, lawyers, divorce attorneys, business managers, and family offices. Develop follow-up strategies because the money is in the follow up. I commend you for investing in your career by reading this book. I call it the principle of slight edge. You are definitely going to get a lot of information nuggets from each chapter that you can implement into your business that your competition doesn't know about.

Now let's get back to your mindset. I can promise you that you will not double your income or be the "rock star" luxury agent in your marketplace if you don't have a strong inner game. Finish this sentence with me, "Garbage in, garbage ..." No, it's not "garbage in, garbage out." That's what most people think. That thought should finish with "garbage stays." Do you realize by the time someone turns 18 they have been told something negative over 100,000 times in their life? That's hearing something negative about 15 times per day. "No, you can't do that. You won't do that. No, stop. No, no, no." We all hear those words a lot, don't we? In that same 18 years, someone has been encouraged only about 2 times a day. That is a lot of negativity to hear, so no wonder the garbage that comes in, stays unfortunately. When you are focused on your goals and your reasons for wanting success, you will surround yourself with positive people. Your environment will be positive. Your inner game will be stronger because you will have a better support system. Work hard to allow all the garbage you hear, all the negative comments or thoughts, to just fall out of your head. Affirmations are one way you can work to overcome negativity. Affirmations work. Like Lisa Hayes says, "Be careful how you are talking to yourself because you are listening." Take that thought to heart and be mindful of what you tell yourself.

There are a few ways you can strengthen your inner game, strengthen yourself esteem, and how you look at yourself. You can do that by eating right, getting proper exercise and enough sleep. Work to improve your self-image. How do you look at yourself? Practice self-confidence and self-discipline. Those are key components to strengthening your inner game and your mindset. Keep only positive, supportive people around you and remove toxicity from your life. All of these components can help keep you focused on what is important.

Once you're in a good place personally, it's time to focus on building your knowledge. There are several levels to increase your knowledge as an agent. You need to increase your knowledge about your company, your clients, your competition, and what gives you the competitive advantage over other agents. You also need to be able to articulate this information to both potential and current clients. I will discuss finding your unique selling proposition later. This involves building excellent people skills, being likable, and being influential. You should also have expansive knowledge of the local, regional, national, and international real estate markets. Finally, build your knowledge on sales skills. Grow your knowledge, practice that knowledge, and your confidence will grow. Your inner game will grow. You'll take more risks, and you'll be more confident because you have the knowledge and skills on which to rely.

Your environment can be toxic or supportive. There are two types of people in this world: people that drag you down and those that pull you up. It's often very clear which people are positive or negative. Consider the media, what's on the Internet, the radio, television, and in newspapers. Is the information positive or negative? Much more often than not, the information we consume is extremely negative. This is just another example of the idea "Garbage in, garbage stays." Many times, we become so numb to the negativity in the world that we don't realize how it af-

fects our lives and our success in business. Don't succumb to the garbage. Separate your business and your goals from the garbage in the world and focus on bringing everything positive to your work.

The problem with most agents is that they have limiting beliefs. If you say, "I don't have enough experience" guess what? You're not going to take action because you have discounted yourself from even having a chance. If you don't take action, you're never going to know what you're capable of, nor will you gain the experience necessary to build your confidence and sales power. When you have never "gone out there" and taken action, you maintain the assumption that you're not good enough to compete in the luxury market. Don't sell yourself short. You have to strengthen your inner game and face challenges head on. With time and hard work, your business and your mindset will improve tremendously.

Look at this idea in terms of the proverbial baseball analogy. You can't hit a home run if you don't get up to bat. Of course, the more at-bats you have, yes, you'll strike out more, but getting more at-bats also means it is more likely that you will get hits, even home runs, and become more successful. The problem is that most people never step into the batter's box because they're afraid of striking out. They're afraid of failure. They're afraid of what someone might say. They're afraid of how they might look if they make a mistake. They're simply afraid of trying. You're never going to be successful if you are afraid of others and their thoughts. My mentor Dan Kennedy once said, "Whether someone said something good about you or bad about you, take it as a compliment." Have no fear, just do it, and don't worry about what other people think. Like Babe Ruth said, "Never let the fear of striking out keep you from playing the game." Take this reference to heart and remember it when you feel uncertain about a new challenge.

I want to share one other athletic reference with you to illustrate the importance of a positive mindset. Roger Bannister was the first person to

run the mile under four minutes. Well, guess what? Within two years of his accomplishment, there were 37 other runners that broke the 4-minute-mile barrier. It wasn't because Nike came out with better shoes or Gatorade was developed. It was the inner belief of those athletes. They realized the barrier was broken, the bar was set, and they believed if Roger Bannister could run the mile in under four minutes, they could too. Apply that mentality to business. If Michael LaFido, a guy that scored a 19 on his ACT can become successful and achieve lofty career goals, so can you.

Let's talk about action steps next. I want you to implement these things, and when you do, you will experience results. First, figure out your "why" for wanting to build your business and enjoy more success. You need to have lots of visuals and have constant reminders. Your "why" is what motivates you and keeps you moving forward when you experience setbacks. You need to strengthen your brain and your inner game with good books, masterminds, and other successful people. Strengthening your inner game is so important. Then you have to decide what your business model is. You need to have three goals that you work to achieve each day. Develop steps to reach these goals and chip away at them incrementally. Once you develop your business model and your goals, you have armed yourself with a plan and have set yourself up for positive growth and improvement.

What Would A 30% Raise Do in the Next Year for Your Business

Elevated Price Point		
Average Sale Price	Increase 30%	Average Sale Price
$200,000	⇨	$260,000
$300,000	⇨	$390,000
$500,000	⇨	$650,000
$750,000	⇨	$975,000

Misconceptions (Limiting Beliefs) About Selling Luxury Homes

- You Must Be A Top Producer Or Veteran Agent Before You Sell High-End Homes
- You Personally Need To Be Wealthy
- You Personally Need To Live In A Big Home
- You Personally Need To Drive A Nice Car
- You Personally Need To Be With A Certain Office

Good News For You

- There Are Lots Of "Traditional" Agents
- There Are Lots Of "Dinosaur" Agents

Get Out Of Your Comfort Zone

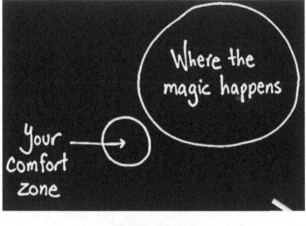

7 Levels Of Knowledge

1. Knowledge Of Your Company
2. Knowledge Of Your Client
3. Knowledge Of Your Competition
4. Knowledge Of What Gives You The Advantage & Being Able To Articulate It
5. Knowledge Of Local, Regional, National, and International Real Estate Markets
6. People Skills/Being Likable/Influence
7. Sales Skills

Grow Your Knowledge & Your Confidence Will Grow

All Potential Clients Care About

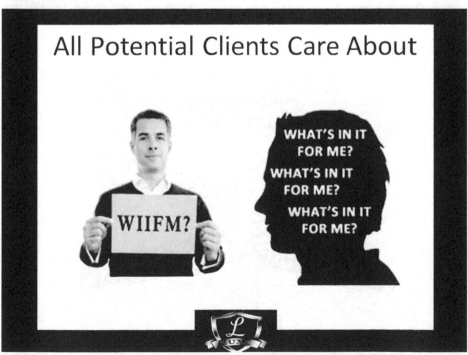

Garbage In, Garbage...

IN   OUT

Garbage In = Garbage Stays

The Problem With Most Agents

Can't Hit A Home Run If You Don't Step Into The Batter's Box. The More At Bats, The More Likely You'll Get A Home Run

Why Not You?

Roger Bannister-May 6, 1954

Within 2 years, 37 others runners broke the 4-minute-mile barrier

"Shock & Awe Package"

"Hunger is a prerequisite for success."

- Michael LaFido

LUXURY LISTING SPECIALIST PODCAST

CHAPTER 3 | How to Close More Deals by Mastering Personality Types

"If you hang out with 9 broke people, you're bound to be the 10th."

- Zig Ziglar

As I discussed in the previous chapter, there are three ways to double your income this year. One of them is to sell more homes. Maybe you don't need to go on more appointments to boost your business and earn higher income. You just need to increase your conversion, and one of the ways you can do that is understanding and mastering personality profiles and mirroring behaviors to connect with clients. There are a lot of good personality profile programs to learn from such as Myers Briggs and Kolbe.

DISC is the one type of personality profile that a lot of real estate companies and agents use. Each letter represents a personality category that clients, colleagues, and other business professionals fall under. Figuring out a person's personality is an excellent way to learn the best way to successfully communicate with him or her, ultimately leading to a beneficial professional relationship.

The **D** stands for dominant. The **I** stands for influencing. The **S** stands for supportive, and the **C** stands for cautious.

D: The D's are fast-paced and outspoken. They're inquisitive and competitive. They're often skeptical, and they want to win. This personality type is often very successful, but be careful not to be too authoritative and domineering in business dealings. An example of that personality type is Michael Jordan.

I: The I's are influencers. They're also fast-paced, social, and outspoken. In a conversation, they won't let you get a word in. Ironically, this is not the most effective personality for a real estate agent, but it's probably the most common personality type of real estate agents. For many agents, it seems natural to talk, and then talk more. To communicate well with clients, we need to slow down and listen. We need to listen to find out what they need and how we can help them. As agents, we need to be accepting and warm. An example of the influencer personality type is Dolly Parton.

S: The S is supportive. They're accepting and warm. These are very sincere individuals who relate well to all types of people. They're known as congenial and are good listeners. The "S" personality type is also a great team player and has tremendous patience, both outstanding qualities to have in a colleague. However, as an agent who is a supportive personality type, you need to make sure you're standing your ground and not coming across as passive in your business dealings. A famous supportive personality example is Michelle Obama.

C: They're cautious and reflective. The "C" personality type is often a perfectionist who has very high standards and aims to be as methodical and accurate as possible. These people are data and fact finders who pay attention to detail. If you are a "C" personality, you might be a bit sensitive as well, so be sure to protect yourself and your clients who represent these traits. If you have ever watched the classic TV series *The Odd Couple*, Felix Unger is a perfect example of a cautious personality.

Let me give you a quick example to illustrate how influential personality types can be on interaction. I'm going to use an airport story. Here's how the different personality types would handle the situation if they were running late to the airport. If someone with the "dominant" personality was running late to the airport they would be frantic. It would drive them crazy to feel any loss of control or not see results. They'd probably be rude to some people because of their stress, saying things like "You have to get me on this plane." They'd probably cut in line at TSA and barge through crowds to get to a gate. These types of people are not worried about others, just focused on themselves. They aren't necessarily trying to be this way because that's just how they think. So, next time you hear someone at a service desk say, "You have to get me on this plane. Do you know who I am?" Know that he or she is very likely a dominant personality.

The "influencers" want to socialize. They're really nice, and they would attract people with honey as the saying goes, always very sweet. They'd talk. They'd give compliments. Somehow, they'd get to the front of the line and maybe talk themselves onto the plane.

Let's contrast that with the "supportive" personality type. They're great people, but they don't like confrontation, so an "S" person would probably not say anything in this airport scenario. They'd stand at the back of the line. They wouldn't speak up. If something was wrong with their food at a restaurant, they wouldn't ask that the meat or steak be taken back to be cooked a little bit more. They just don't like confrontation. They're content being supportive. They're great listeners, and that "S" person would not get on that plane if they were running late because they wouldn't want to speak up.

Finally, let's discuss the "cautious" individual in the airport. The "C" person is analytical and very organized. That "C" would be there two hours before the flight was scheduled to leave because they want to elimi-

nate the risk of missing the flight due to heavy traffic, long lines, or any other unexpected travel snafu. The "C" people are also very left-brained thinkers: analytical and linear. They want to verify and double check everything. So, the "C" person wouldn't have to worry about missing the flight because they would be there on time. So, again, the airport scenario is a great way to determine what personality type someone fits into.

It's important to be aware of personality profiles with negotiations as well. If I'm an agent representing the seller, I need to know what my seller's personality type is when negotiating with them and for them. However, I also need to know the personality type of the buyer's agent. If they're dominant, only wanting to know the bottom-line and wanting to win, they're going to be a combative negotiator. So, I need to build them up. I need to make them feel like they won even though I'm actually getting something in return. I just structure the conversation and negotiating in a way that flatters the other agent. In terms of negotiating style, there are collaborative and competitive negotiators. Competitive negotiators just want to want to win. These individuals tend to be a "D" or a "C" personality type. The "I" and the "S" negotiators tend to be more collaborative and often are willing to work with the other side to reach terms everyone is happy with. These situations specifically illustrate why understanding personality types in negotiation is crucial to be successful in this business.

Again, certain personality types and groups of people buy differently. They think differently, which means their buying buttons are different. Their communication style is also very different. You need to know that because that's how you build rapport quickly with your clients. Theodore Roosevelt once said, "Nobody cares how much you know, until they know how much you care." That is exactly how your clients need to feel when they talk to you. They should feel like you're listening to them, that you hear them, that you understand what's important to them. That's how they know they can trust you to help them find what they're looking

for. How do you do that? You must quickly observe them and through identify their personality type because it will dictate the way they handle every step of the transaction.

When you're working with a buyer, understanding personality types is also important. Consider this example. "Mister buyer, when I set up appointments and we go look at homes, do you want to look at all the homes quickly and just circle back to the homes you really like? I understand your time is valuable, so I don't want to waste it touring homes that are not viable options for you." That approach would be a "D" or an "I" style communication. An "S" or "C" person might say, "Or do you want us to look at each home thoroughly and take our time? I know this is a big decision and we want to be sure we see everything that could possibly work for you."

Another way you can use personality knowledge to your advantage is to develop **three types of listing presentations.** You should have a bottom-line type of presentation for the "D" and "I" clients. It's faster-paced, gets to the point, goes over your prices, your packages, maybe a quick video to show them what makes you different. Give the clients all the information in a quick, professional manner and that's it. You should have a slower-paced presentation as well. This is more detail-oriented and better suited for the "S" and the "C" individuals within the DISC personality categories. With these clients, you need to explain line by line and show them the paperwork ahead of time so they can have their attorney review it. You might want to have more visuals and more graphs to reference during your presentation. You must back up your points with data. You need to cite your sources and your references. Practice peaking slower because you'll need to allow them more time for processing. You should also work on being aware of your tone. Various personality types interpret the way you say things even when you may not realize any difference.

There will be instances when you have to gear your presentation to more than one personality type at a time. This situation calls for the "mixed presentation." For example, maybe the husband is a "D" or an "I" and the wife is an "S" or a "C" or vice versa. You will be speaking to them at the same time in many cases, and you definitely want to cater to both. To determine how to proceed, figure out who seems to have the "final say" in the decision-making process. That role changes for every household. Once you know that important factor, two thirds of your presentation should be geared toward the decision-maker and his or her personality type, and one third should cater to the other person.

All right, now let's conclude this chapter with action steps to help you put this information to use in your business. First, I want you to take a DISC personality profile to determine where you fall within the categories we have discussed. There are a lot of different sites to use, and you can Google "free DISC personality profile." You're going to have a primary result and a secondary result. For example, I'm primarily a "D" followed by an "I," which means most of my personality falls under the dominant category. That is critical to know because it influences every aspect of my business and communication. Figure out what your primary and secondary categories are, and then figure out your significant other's personality type (great support system for practice), and then you need to develop your three different types of listing presentations.

Airport Story

- **D** – Wants to Win, Get Results
- **I** – Wants to Socialize, Influence
- **S** – Wants to Connect, Support
- **C** – Wants to Process, Verify

"When we get feedback from agents that have showed your home, do you want me to go over the feedback with you quickly and just bottom line it for you… or would you rather me to take my time and go through each feedback response thoroughly?"

Master Personality Types

D
DOMINANT
Determined
Demanding
Driving
Doers

I
INFLUENCING
Impressive
Interactive
Inspiring
Initiators

C
CAUTIOUS
Competent
Creative
Curious
Coordinators

S
SUPPORTIVE
Sensitive
Steady
Stable
Servants

Sell The Way THEY Want To Be Sold

- The <u>Golden Rule- (25%)</u>

Treat others the way you want to be treated

- The <u>Platinum Rule- (100%)</u>

Treat others the way THEY want to be treated

This is the fastest way to be respected while gaining trust.

3 Presentations

- Bottom-Line Presentation (D/I)

  -faster paced/get to the point/price/packages
- Detail Oriented (S/C)

  -line by line/graphs/back things up w/sources

  -speak slower/allow time for processing
- Mixed Presentation (D/I & S/C)

  -balance of both. Figure out who is the decision maker and present more toward them

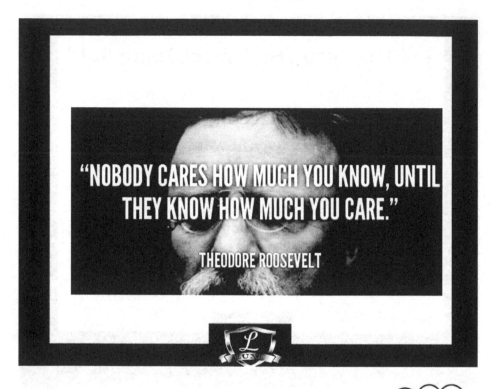

Retention After 3 Days

It's starting to make sense now.

WHICH REALTOR IS BEST FOR **YOU?**

"From what I was told in Real Estate School"

"The numbers's in my spreadsheet never lie"

Part-Timer Patty - (60% of Agents)

Pros: 1 - Cheap
2 - Will do whatever you tell them to do
3 - Won't be calling everyday

Cons: 1 - Only available before/after other job
2 - No systems
3 - Doesn't answer phone calls, texts or emails in a timely manner

Ideal for: Non-motivated or unrealistic sellers

Analytical Alex - (10% of Agents)

Pros: 1 - Great with numbers
2 - Great at writing lengthy emails
3 - Organized

Cons: 1 - Not creative
2 - Weaker communication skills
3 - Would rather email than return calls

Ideal for: Sellers that believe the home will sell itself b/c of the details

"I'm available to grab coffee or talk 24/7 about anything/everything"

"Massive exposure & marketing is how I sell homes faster & for more money"

Chatty Cathy - (25% of Agents)

Pros: 1 - Great communicator
2 - You know what they are thinking
3 - Will host open house every weekend

Cons: 1 - Unorganized
2 - No marketing systems
3 - Believes "word of mouth" will sell your home

Ideal for: Seller who believe their home will sell because of "word of mouth marketing"

Marketer Matthew - (5% of Agents)

Pros: 1 - Strong negotiating skills
2 - Outside the box thinking
3 - Uses proven systems
4 - Knows what really sells homes

Cons: 1 - Won't be easily swayed
2 - On the move & always improving
3 - Doesn't like to be micromanaged

Ideal for: The owner who hires the best & will entrust experts to do the job

Not Pictured: Debbie Dinosaur & Newbie Nathan

"Attract vs. chase is the name of the game in the luxury market."

- Michael LaFido

**LUXURY
LISTING
SPECIALIST
PODCAST**

LUXE
LUXURY LISTING
SPECIALIST

CHAPTER 4 | How to Identify the Perfect Buyers for Your Listings

"Whatever you do, do it well. Do it so well that when people see you do it they will want to come back and see you do it again..."
- Walt Disney

It's important to know who your potential buyer is when marketing a luxury home. You need to identify who your buyer is and be strategically focusing on marketing your message to those buyers, and even those agents that work with buyers you want to reach. Once this crucial step is complete, you will want to articulate the unique features and benefits of the home you are marketing to potential buyers through your descriptions, pictures, and any type of video marketing you orchestrate. For example, if the home you are marketing has a seven-car garage, you might consider bringing in a muscle car or a couple of classic cars to highlight that incredible garage because these features carry significant clout for car collectors and can help you identify target buyers. In this example, we would do our research and compile a list of potential buyers, and we would also develop a list of business owners who cater to those car aficionados and have relationships with our potential buyers.

We would then market the home to potential luxury buyers who have lived in their homes for five or more years, and who also have an interest in luxury and classic cars. We would use a similar process if the home we are marketing is situated on a lake. We would, of course, want to capture the lifestyle of living in a home that backs to a beautiful lake through photos, descriptions, and videos of the home. Then put together a marketing plan to target potential buyers that are avid fishermen and boaters. Determining who the potential buyer is starts by focusing on both the home and the amenities the property and surrounding areas have to

offer. Next, strategically focus marketing and message to potential buyers and agents locally as well as globally.

A marketing topic that is not discussed as much is learning migration patterns. As a savvy agent, you should know if there are certain corporations that are moving people in or out of town. Keep an eye on business in the area because there is a lot of potential to connect with executives and other high-level professionals who are moved around more than you might realize. Try to build a relationship with companies' relocation co-ordinators and buyers' agents that work with these people. Identify key cities that they're moving from. In many cities, additional opportunities are available with professional athletic teams. The first step to "get in" with these groups is to call around and find a contact. Then work to build a relationship with that person to build trust and showcase the unparalleled services you have to offer.

In this chapter, the most critical action step I can give you is to know your buyer. Knowing the preferences of buyers in your marketplace is a critical key to success when planning your approach to marketing the home you are working to sell. Don't let your likes, tastes, or preferences influence your strategies. Rather, be objective and pay attention to what buyers want at that time, sort of a "what's hot and what's not" mindset. If you gear your efforts to the demands of the market, you will sell that home much more quickly, a win for both you and your clients.

Most Listened To Radio Station

What's In It For Me (WIIFM)?
Prospects Only Care About Themselves,
Their Time, Their Money

- What do you do to solve their problems?
- Will you save them time?
- Will you save them aggravation?
- Will you save them money?

Who Is Your Buyer?

- Identify target buyers
- Strategically focus marketing and message to potential buyers
- Don't "list" the home before the "to-do" list is complete
- Only one chance to make a lasting first impression
- Don't undervalue your luxury properties

GET MORE LUXURY CLIENTS NOW

If YOU want to get attention and stand out and become a trusted person of influence, you **NEED** this certification **RIGHT NOW** to gain an unfair advantage and competitive edge to promote and market your business, reach celebrity status, attract better customers, make more money, and help a lot of people.

To learn more on how to get certified visit:
www.LuxuryListingSpecialist.com

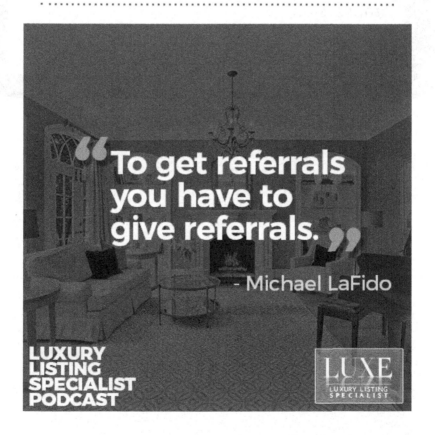

CHAPTER 5 | How NOT Knowing Your Numbers Is Costing You More Than Money

"Rich people have big libraries. Poor people have big TVs."

- Dan Kennedy

What do you know about the luxury market in your area? Most agents make a colossal mistake by not educating their sellers on the facts of their real estate market from the beginning of the relationship and continuing throughout the transaction. Not managing the seller's expectations from the get-go is probably the number-one mistake that I see agents make when marketing a high-end home. On the other hand, those sellers also make a colossal mistake by not knowing the facts about their market before proceeding with selling their home. This is the primary reason why the sale fails and sellers end up with no showings or offers.

One of the most important things you can do as an agent is to educate your clients on global real estate trends as well as your local market. Unless you are in a cookie-cutter neighborhood with similar homes that include similar finishes, determining the asking price of a luxury home is very difficult. The unique features luxury homes have to offer can dramatically influence the asking price and how long it takes to sell the home. Most sellers and real estate agents operate in the dark. They simply enter the marketplace at a certain price without identifying the other homes in the area that are direct competition for potential buyers.

Another way you need to educate your clients is through sharing data. You need to know whether it's a buyer's or seller's market for each of the price points in the markets you service, and you need to know the average number of days on the market. Some other data you need to share

with your clients is the list of sale prices and their ratios to list prices, plus other factors that influence the sale of a home. You simply need to do your due diligence in your market before listing a high-end home. Do all the work so your sellers don't have to worry, and be thorough so they feel confident in their decision to work with you on this major transaction. Now you might wonder why it is so important to educate your clients. Don't they just want to sell their house? Why do they need to know the market data? The biggest reason is because there is a lot of misleading information online regarding real estate.

It has created some difficult problems for agents and their clients because many of these real estate sites are inaccurate, and agents have to "correct" that information. The reality in today's marketplace is that consumers have access to just about every property for sale with numerous websites like Zillow, Redfin, and Realtor.com. This allows consumers to "window shop" by viewing multiple photos and descriptions of every property in the price range. However, these sites do not provide an accurate opinion of value, and it doesn't take a rocket scientist to figure out that when a property offers fewer amenities and upgrades than the competition but is priced the same, that it is overpriced. These pricing mistakes turn into frustration and long months on the market for sellers. The accurate information is not usually what buyers or sellers want to believe, but as their agent, it is your job to arm them with the right information.

Online Home Value Estimate

For example, I have recently conducted a study on 10 of the highest priced homes for sale in Illinois. I compared the asking prices of the 10 homes for sale to a well-known website that let's consumers know the home's estimated value.

Well, after reviewing the numbers, the owners for some of these homes may not be too happy. In today's modern world, a lot of

buyers look to online value websites as the Kelley Blue Book of real estate. But the truth is that online value sites simply aren't accurate enough for this to be the case. At the end of the day, the market determines value—not online value sites. Sellers should always rely on an appraisal for the most accurate information possible. But let's get back to those 10 properties I mentioned earlier. As it turns out, 9 out of the 10 online values were priced well below asking price. This doesn't entirely surprise me. What did surprise me, though, was that 8 of the 10 properties had a online value that came up to just 43 percent or less of the true asking price. Also, 1 of the 10 online estimates valued a home at just 1 percent of its asking price. That's a huge difference. Of the 10 homes I looked at, only 1 actually had a favorable online value that was above asking price. So, at least in the case of high-end homes, do not rely on online value sites to determine the value of your property. Online values are simply way off.

THE MACRO VIEW OF THE MARKET

When you price a home appropriately, it will sell much more quickly and sell closer to list price. So what can you do to ensure your sellers price their home right? Potential real estate sellers need to think about three specific areas to determine correct pricing:

- Criteria one is the overview of the general market in your area.
- The second criteria is how your specific property stacks up against the competition in the market.
- Third criteria is the amount of time you have available to achieve the goal of selling your home.

For example, if your prevailing local market conditions are such that the number of sellers far outweigh the number of buyers and you have only

a month to get your home sold, you will obviously need great marketing efforts and aggressive pricing, along with avoiding mistakes, to get to the closing table quickly. Furthermore, if your property lacks uniqueness, then creativity and active marketing outside of the box, along with physical improvements to the property, will certainly be necessary.

DETERMINING ASKING PRICE - *ADVICE FOR AGENTS*

Before we get into establishing the value of your particular property, it is important to take an overview of surrounding market conditions. Getting the macro view data is something that you can ask of a real estate appraiser since they often use this information anyway.

DAYS ON MARKET (DOM) INDICATOR

The average days on market data is critical for several reasons:

- It is important in setting realistic expectations about the time needed to sell a home.
- It will help you evaluate any pending offer and make an educated decision about whether it's advisable to wait for another offer or take what is being offered on the table.
- If you know the DOM for your market (or, better yet, for the specific neighborhood), you'll be able to make a better decision on pricing and negotiate accordingly.

There is a major problem with DOM statistics, however. Most MLS databases have a very inaccurate DOM number, which is invariably skewed lower than the actual real-world number. So how can you know what the real number is? Is it possible to determine? Absolutely! You can arrive at the accurate number by using the absorption method (which I will explain next) to calculate the true DOM for your area.

Let's talk about why the DOM number in the MLS is a lie. You may ask why there is such a huge disparity in the actual DOM number versus the reported number? The MLS calculates the average DOM as the average days on the market only for the homes that actually sold. As I stated previously, the MLS completely leaves out homes that are withdrawn, homes that expired, homes that were withdrawn and relisted (which restarts the clock, a typical real estate agent trick to make a home look like it just became available), or those that were never put into the MLS until they sold. This often happens with new construction homes where agents or developers might list only one home in a subdivision, but actually have 400 for sale. All of these factors affect the calculation of the real DOM number.

ABSORBTION RATE *EXTREMELY VALUABLE INFORMATION*

The absorption rate is an extremely useful indicator of supply and demand for homes in your area. The absorption rate is simply a ratio of the number of homes for sale in your area divided by the number of closings in the last 30 days. I typically define "area" as a school district, since the school district often determines how desirable a particular area is. This measure helps you estimate the number of months it would take to sell a home. Understanding the absorption rate and its trend over the last few months (whether trending up or down) can make sellers tens of thousands of dollars and save a great deal of time. The absorption rate is to a seller what GPS-guided navigation is to a driver! It is hard to imagine navigating the housing market without this critical statistic. Knowing your absorption rate is the first step toward the right mindset to getting a home sold within a particular time period.

AVERAGE MARKDOWN *LIST PRICE vs. SALE PRICE*

Next, you need to be aware of the typical "discount" in your market. This is just like in car sales when you compare the sticker price on a vehicle to what you walk out the door paying for it. Let's look at how this plays out in real estate:

For this exercise, assume an average list price in your market for a luxury home is $3,500,000 and the average sale price of $3,338,000. Subtract the average sale price from the average list price, and then divide the difference by the average home price.

Here's the math: $3,500,000-$3,338,000 = $162,000.
$162,000 divided by $3,500,000 = 0.046 or a 4.6 percent markdown.

In other words, for this example you should understand that it's normal in your market to expect a discount of 4.6 percent from the home's list price. **Do you know the average list price to sale price ratio in your market?** You'll also have an advantage in negotiations with other agents when you know the average markdown. Luxury homes tend to sell at a larger markdown, **so when you have done the math and have the numbers to back up your negotiations, you can work out a better deal for your clients.**

In terms of action steps, it is critical for you as the agent to manage your client's expectations from day one. For you to be effective at this skill, you need to be able to articulate market data and market trends, as well as global influences and how that will affect your client's sale price and how long they should expect the home to be on the market before selling. Not knowing your numbers will not only cost you money but could also cost you clients and your reputation; furthermore, your reputation could then affect your overall business growth and success.

Research

- Research the Prospective Client
  - Social Media Scrub
    - Similar Connections
    - Likes and Interests
    - Listed Previously
      - Glaring Deficiencies

Two Options When Selling

1. Option A: "As Is"
   *Easier Path
   *Less Stressful Initially
   *"Cheaper" But Sellers Net Less Money
2. Option B: Small Investment (maybe larger)
   *Pro-Active & Address "Elephants"...Verify?
   *Car Metaphor (Certified Pre-Owned)
   *Invest Money To Make Money
   *Home Will Sell Faster & Sellers Will Net More
   Money At Closing

Know The #'s & Yours

Use Great Visuals-

Most People Are Terrible At Math

- Buyer's Or Seller's Market?
- List To Sale Ratio
- Number Of Months of Inventory
- Sales Rate (% of Homes That Sell)

Months Supply's Impact on Price

Months	Market	Pricing
1-4	Sellers	Appreciation
5-6	Even	The Norm
7+	Buyers	Depreciation

"It Doesn't Matter If You And I Think Your Home Is Worth____... Or, For That Matter, What A Website Says Your Home Is Worth. All That Matters Is What Buyers Think Your Home Is Worth."

"If you are just looking to throw it on the MLS, it's going to be a stale luxury property."

- Michael LaFido

LUXURY LISTING SPECIALIST PODCAST

CHAPTER 6 | Why Pro-Active Selling Is a Must in a Buyer's Market

"Insanity is doing the same thing over and over again and expecting different results."
                                                    - Albert Einstein

PROACTIVE vs. REACTIVE SELLING

In this chapter, we are going to talk about the benefits of being proactive versus reactive when working with the seller. When marketing a home, especially a luxury home, it is important to step back and think like a skeptical buyer. Take away your emotions and put your personal biases aside, and think like a skeptical buyer. Being proactive means taking action and maintaining control of your plan, rather than reactive, which is simply reacting to what others do. Being proactive will position the home more effectively in the market and increase the profitability for a quicker sale at top dollar.

Being reactive seems like the better option at first because it doesn't address potential roadblocks or create any unnecessary stress. It's the easier path. It could be less stressful and it's also cheaper, initially, but in the end, it's going to cause more stress and cost sellers money. We want to make sure that doesn't happen. Now let's discuss option two, a proactive approach. There's a small initial investment, which sellers might balk at. You're proactively addressing the elephants in the room, picking out issues that could arise and tackling them head-on. Sellers invest money in their homes to make money, not spend money. It's not an "expense" because it's an "investment" in this transaction and plan to sell the house for top dollar. This reverse engineering approach has saved my clients hundreds of thousands of dollars and has removed red flags and excuses from potential buyers and other agents. These factors ultimately con-

vince the buyer to select your client's home versus the competition. Being proactive is also beneficial in the negotiation process as it saves time and money.

Think about this: Have you ever gone shopping for a used car? Why do car buyers pay a premium for a Mercedes-Benz or BMW certified pre-owned luxury automobile instead of buying those used cars from a private party? The answer is that they have peace of mind through transparency and warranties. They know the history and condition of the vehicle they're investing in, so they should not experience any surprise issues that will inconvenience them and cost money. Customers are willing to pay extra money to buy peace of mind. For example, Mercedes' pre-owned cars offer a 164-point pre-inspection to ease buyers' anxieties. If it's priced at or below Kelley Blue Book value and future service visits and a warranty are included, apprehensions about purchasing are lessened. It's pretty simple, and certainly understandable. People will pay a premium for this car versus buying it privately because its history has been verified as opposed to the many unknowns that accompany purchase from a private seller. This same method applies to real estate. The benefits of being proactive and investing in some services outweigh any initial cost. Consider the value of peace of mind for both buyers and sellers, and do what you can to provide that for them.

Now, what exactly can you do as an agent to be proactive? Think like a buyer and take a fresh-eyes analysis of your listings. Are there any "elephants in the room" for the home that you are marketing? Does the home that you are marketing have deferred maintenance items or dated features? If so, you have a few options:

- Address any areas of concern that need to be updated or fixed. Be tactful and sensitive to the seller's feelings, but be honest. You're only trying to help them.

- Credit the buyers at closing so they can address those areas that need to be updated or fixed.

- Price the home lower because of the lack of updating or differed maintenance. Market research shows that it is always better to fix and update items before going to marketplace versus just giving the buyer a credit. You need to invest money in the right places to make money.

- The reality is that buyers will discount their offer even more if the seller doesn't address the issues.

WHAT ARE SOME EXAMPLES OF BEING PROACTIVE?

Each home should be pre-inspected, pre-appraised, a preliminary title report should be pulled, and a home warranty should be provided to the purchaser. For a "Verified Home" the following four services must be performed before going to marketplace:

HOME INSPECTION: BEFORE PUTTING THE HOME ON THE MARKET

Did you know a home inspection is the number-one reason most deals fall apart? A home inspector will find something wrong, or perhaps not up-to-code on the home. Obviously, you would rather have your inspector discover this so you can fix the issue rather than the buyers discovering any issues. Think about that. Why wouldn't you be proactive and invest in a pre-inspection so you are prepared for potential problems that may arise prior to securing a buyer? The alternative is to be reactive and deal with red flags during negotiation or worse, lose the sale. Buyers today are looking for reasons to justify a lowball offer or to not buy the house at all. Many buyers will use inspection issues as a reason to return to the negotiating table and lower the agreed-upon contract price. So, if you can address these issues in advance, you create transparency with potential buyers and differentiate your home from the competition.

Depending on what part of the country you're in, you may also consider getting the following tests done before going to market: a radon test, Dryvit test, termite test, etc. For example, if your listing is in the Midwest and the exterior is stucco or Dryvit, it would be smart to have the sellers get a professional inspection done. If there are issues, take care of them ahead of time and then offer a clean bill of health to potential buyers. This will also create transparency to buyers and help you differentiate your listing from your competitors.

DISCUSS WITH YOUR SELLER

Seller: "What? You're asking me to have an inspection done?"

Agent: "Well, yes, because it is important to differentiate your property. The higher end market is a buyer's market, and one of the ways to differentiate yourself is get a home inspection done."

Seller: "Well, what if something goes wrong during inspection?"

Agent: "That's why it needs to be done. We can identify and get those issues taken care of. It's going to be a lot cheaper to have your handyman fix them versus the buyers requesting a licensed professional. Remember, transparency is a good thing when selling a luxury home."

PRE-APPRAISAL

There are two types of appraisals. One is a bank appraisal for purchase or refinancing, and the other is a private appraisal, where your client hires a company to do an appraisal on the house. Even luxury buyers are concerned with overpaying for a home, so they will research real estate websites like Zillow that provide online home value estimates before

viewing a home in person. Have you looked at your listing's estimated value on Zillow lately? Is the home value where you think it should be? It's probably not, so what I am about to share with you will be crucial. My recommendation is to get the home appraised prior to going on the market if possible. Your buyer will most likely make a relatively large down payment or purchase in cash; however, for peace of mind or to secure a mortgage, they must get a licensed appraisal.

If you can be proactive and have your appraisal done ahead of time you can anticipate the competition from similar homes from your buyer's appraisal. Perhaps you will find out the inside scoop on those comparable properties, the seller's motivation level, and why they sold. This information can be vital to properly defend your listing's asking price. A favorable appraisal can be leveraged and offered to both buyers and agents prior to them viewing the home. For my listings, I will even post it on the local MLS if favorable, because it allows buyers to see what a great deal they're getting before seeing the home. In the case of an unfavorable appraisal, the information will not be disclosed or published on the MLS, but it still arms you with the necessary information to make an educated decision based on the appraised value of the home. It prepares you for an uphill battle to justify the value of the home to potential appraisers when the time comes. In my experience, online value websites severely undervalue luxury homes.

PRELIMINARY TITLE REPORT

With so many short sales, bank and contractor liens on luxury homes throughout the country, it's smart to be proactive and transparent by showing buyers there are no surprises with the home. By delivering a clean title to buyers and agents you will have an edge over reactive competitors. This is yet another way to differentiate your listing from your direct competition.

Once again, think of yourself as that skeptical buyer. Alleviate any extra

stress they may be having during this time and take away potential red flags that could prevent them from making an offer on the house. There are a few other tasks that I recommend as well, like offering an extended home warranty, touch up painting, staging, professional cleaning, landscaping, and neutralizing the home. As I mentioned before, if the home's exterior is covered with stucco or Dryvit and you live in the Midwest, getting inspections and/or a warranty on your exterior before going on the market gives peace of mind to buyers and takes possible objections off the table. Another reason I strongly recommend these strategies is because they will also create transparency for buyers. These are just some of the things you can do to create peace of mind and differentiate your listing from the competition.

How can you be proactive? *Let's go over your action steps.* Before your listing goes on the market, you need to get a pre-inspection done. You should get a preliminary title and recommend that your clients offer a home warranty. You should also have an appraisal done. Those are the four majors, but additionally, you can have other inspections done like a Dryvit inspection, a termite inspection, and an inspection on the pool, shake shingles or the slate roof if applicable, and the boat dock if the home is on water. Remember, time is money, and for your buyer, primarily high-net-worth individuals, time is money as well. By prepaying for some of these maintenance services, it's a way to differentiate your client's home from the competition on the market.

Systematize your pre-listing to-do list that you need to do as an agent and a brokerage to be proactive. Put it on a checklist so that you're consistently doing these things on all your listings. Also, give your sellers a list of things to do. Sellers can make more money and have less stress overall by being proactive and their home will sell faster. If they understand that, they will not fight you on these additional investments and some extra work to get the home ready to sell.

With that being said, it is important for you to stress the benefits of being proactive to your sellers so that your home stands above the competition. Put together your proactive team of service providers and integrate them into your listing presentation so that it won't be a surprise to your clients once you have hired them.

Proactive ☑

Reactive ☐

Information Gathering

- Pre-listing Checklist
- Outside the Home
- Inside the Home
- Updates
- Special Features
- Builder & Architect
- Previous Owners

Buying A Used Car

Car A **Certified** pre-owned

Car B

$41,000

$41,000

- One Year Warranty
- 161 Point Inspection
- Free Oil Changes
- KBB Value Appraised
- New Tires
- Detailed

- As Is

Which would you choose?

Selling Your Car

Car A

Car B

$39,500

$33,500

- New Tires
- Detailed
- Transferable Warranty
- Car History

- As Is

Would You Invest $1,000 to Make $5,000?

How Verified House Works...

Home A

$1,498,000
- Home Warranty Included
- Appraised Ahead Of Time
- Clean Titled
- Pre-Inspected
- Preventative Receipts
- Builder Info

Home B

$1,495,000

- To be negotiated

Which would you choose?

Before Listing The Home Check:

- Listed Before? If Yes, Previous Special Feature Sheets
- Information On Builders And Architect
- Has The Home Been Featured In Publications?
- MLS Glaring Mistakes
- Buyer's or Seller's Market
- Online Pricing Valuations
- Taxes High?
- Seller Application Returned?

Prepare Your Online & Offline Marketing

- Brochures & Mailings
- Video
- Virtual Tour
- Marketing Materials
- Special Features
- Property Feature Cards
- Website
- Social Media Campaign
- Etc.

Migration Patterns

- Analytics (Know The #'s)
- Corporations Moving In
- Relocation (CEO types)
- Buyer's Agents
- Identify Key Cities
- Professional Teams

Differentiate In With A Pre-Appraisal

 ## Appraisal Challenges

Seller's
Possible Perception of Value

Buyer's
Possible Perception of Value

Appraiser's
Possible Perception of Value

Preliminary Title

1. Differentiate
2. Save The Seller Time
3. Save The Seller Money
4. Give Buyers Peace Of Mind

*View Sample
Title Search
Report*

" **If you do the same things as everyone else, you'll get the same results as everyone else.** "

— Michael LaFido

LUXURY LISTING SPECIALIST PODCAST

CHAPTER 7 | How to Motivate Sellers to Stage Their Home

"You are the average of the five people you spend the most time with."

- Jim Rohn

Staging is crucial to success when selling. Staging is defined as "the act of preparing a private residence for sale in the real estate marketplace. Don't try to cut corners if you decide to stage the home. Sellers need to invest the money in staging, which will ultimately help them net more money at the closing table when the home is sold. Unfortunately, staging is an unregulated industry, so as the agent, you need to make sure that you are only working with the best stagers. The goal of staging is to make a home appeal to the highest number of potential buyers, thereby selling a property more swiftly and for more money." If you watch HGTV, you know staging a home when selling is not optional anymore, especially for luxury home selling.

Only 10 percent of buyers today can visualize beyond the current décor. In other words, 90 percent of buyers view the home as it currently looks with clutter, wallpaper, and any other personal decorative features. The potential buyers cannot imagine their families living there with the current owner's personal decorating style. They just don't have the vision to see what it could be–they only see what is there. That can pose some serious challenges in selling the house because it causes hesitation for buyers who just imagine work and costly updates. Consequently, pictures taken and posted on the Internet and the MLS with dated furniture, wallpaper, or empty rooms prevent 90 percent of buyers from mentally moving into the home. The way I have my own home decorated, or the way you have your home decorated is personalized to individual

taste, and that is great. However, when marketing a home to sell, you need to stage that home to appeal to the majority of buyers based on what market research identifies as most desirable. **Again, it doesn't matter what you think of the home. What matters is what buyers think.** Effective staging targets what buyers are looking for based on countless hours of market research and consumer surveys.

Professionally staged homes consistently sell faster and for more money. Have you ever been in a new construction model home and fallen in love with it? Then, the builder representative takes you to the same model next door or across the street that is empty and it feels completely cold, smaller, and cheaper than the same model home. Why is that? Between two identical models, an empty house will appear colder than a staged one and therefore, cheaper, even with the same floor plan and finishes as the staged model home. It's simple: A little bit of color warms up the space and makes a home more inviting. The staged furniture accentuates the most effective use of spaces and emphasizes the home's special features. Effective staging will help potential buyers develop an emotional attachment to the home and begin imagining themselves living there.

When working with your sellers, is ease of sale and fewer hoops to jump through more attractive to them, or is selling for top dollar their highest priority? If top dollar is their answer (which it almost always is), then always professionally stage the home before listing, and even before the pictures are taken or the sellers will be leaving a lot of money on the table. You will want to articulate your message to your sellers in a delicate way so they don't take offense, because you really need them to listen to your message and suggestions. In this chapter, we're going to be talking about the three types of staging: before and after and a lot of visuals. Barb Schwarz, who many have said is the founder of the term "staging." She defines staging as "the preparation of the home for sale so that buyers can mentally move in, so they can visualize themselves living in that home."

Buyers won't mentally move in unless they actually see the home in person, and they won't even want to see the home in person if the if the photos online are terrible, if the video is terrible, and if the description is lacking. They will decide quickly that they can't see themselves living in that home, so they're not going to request a showing. Being proactive to position the home effectively means taking the time to get the home prepared for its first impression on the market. As we know, the longer the home stays on the market the lower the sale price will be and the seller will have to pay more in carrying costs such as taxes and insurance, etc. Staging is a small investment for sellers to make that will offer a high return on investment.

You never get a second chance to make a first impression. Don't attempt to sell the home as it currently looks and then stage the home after the fact based on lack of activity or feedback. Be proactive. Stage the home before professional photos are taken and put on the MLS. With 92-95 percent of potential buyers starting their search online, photographs are vital to generate interest. If a seller doesn't have the money to invest in professional staging, either do it yourself or possibly offer to pay a portion of the fee.

> "Only 10 percent of buyers can visualize. That is why staging homes to appeal to the majority of buyers' tastes is vital."
>
> - Michael LaFido

Typically, the return on investment from staging is 8-10 percent according to NAR. The primary reason to stage a home is to make its listing photos and videos stand out. Beautiful photos will entice buyers to view the home in person, and when the right buyer comes along, he or she will love the property and make an offer suitable for the value of the

well-appointed home. Our goal in staging a home is that the sellers make more money, the home will sell faster, it's a great return on the investment, and the home will look amazing in both photos and video.

If you need to do some staging on your own for your properties because the sellers are not going to invest in a stager, and if you are not a skilled stager yourself, then there are companies that will virtually stage the home. This is a more affordable but less effective alternative that ultimately affects the sale price. These virtual staging companies will take the photographs provided to them and superimpose furniture and accessories into the pictures. This can be very misleading unless you disclose that the photos have been virtually staged and the home doesn't look like that in reality. I would recommend being extremely cautious if you look into virtual staging. If no other option is available, consider asking a colleague or interior design friend to borrow some pieces and help you stage the home. It is always best for the home to look the same for showings as it does in the photos.

THE FIVE KEYS TO STAGE LIKE A PROFESSIONAL

1. Number one is color. You want to neutralize all colors in the home. You don't want bold colors, and you don't want wallpaper. They both tend to look dated and appeal to a very specific taste. You want to neutralize and make sure the home feels current. From paint colors to furniture colors and accessories, use earth tones. Choose warm colors and soothing colors versus bold. Stay away from anything too bold such as maroon, dark blue, or forest greens. Those are very decorative and very client-specific in terms of taste. You want neutral. Go for light gray, creamy white, beige, or light blue. Those tend to appeal to the majority of buyers.

2. Number two involves depersonalization and decluttering. The fewer distractions the better. You want potential buyers to look at the details of the home, not the owner's personal photos or belongings. Declutter-

ing is essential. Clear items from closets and drawers, organize pantries and cabinets, and keep items picked up while the home is being shown. The purpose of this is to show that the home has plentiful storage and enough room for families of all sizes with many different needs for space.

3. Number three is furniture placement. This is key. You want to create focal points in each room. Strategize the way the home photographs or the way a buyer will walk through the home, and position the furniture accordingly. Additionally, make sure each room shows a purpose. Let buyers know each room is useful, and give them a little help imagining how they will use the space.

4. Number four is all about maintenance. Of course, the home needs to be clean. It needs to smell good. You don't want to have first impressions turn sour if buyers smell something distasteful or flip on a light switch and the bulb is burned out. Everything in the room needs to be working correctly, so complete maintenance checks in all areas inside and out.

5. Number five is giving emotional clues. Help buyers connect with the property through placement of flowers, candles, accessories, and other creative vignettes that tell a story through the home. Buyers also really connect to the way the home smells. That is important–and the reason why many agents bake cookies or burn a vanilla candle before showings and open houses. Those scents trigger an emotional response in buyers that they will remember.

Remember and come back to these five ways to stage like a pro: the color, the depersonalization, furniture placement, maintenance, and emotional clues.

As we have discussed, only 10 percent of buyers can visualize themselves

making preferred changes and moving into a home, while 90 percent can only see the home as it looks online or during the showing. It's our job as agents to articulate to sellers how important it is to be proactive and help buyers visualize themselves moving in by working on the strategies we have discussed.

Here's a sample conversation that can help you approach this topic with your clients: "Mr. Seller, you see, the way you live in your home and the way I live in my home are personalized to our own tastes and our liking. We decorate, we make changes, and we make the house our own so we love it. All of that is wonderful, but when you go to sell your home, you want to neutralize. You want to make sure the home appeals to the masses. You can't be all things to all people, Mr. Seller, but you can be many things to the majority of today's buyers based on market research and what these surveys are telling us."

When you're getting the grand tour of the home and see that the owners have pink wallpaper, say something like "Mr. Seller, I love your pink wallpaper. If I bought your home I would probably not do a darn thing. However, market research suggests that pink is a decorative color and that we should neutralize when you sell."

The following is your recommended course of conversation if the seller disagrees with staging the home.

"Mr. Seller, Einstein defined insanity as doing the same thing over and over again and expecting different results. You told me why you want to sell. You told me you wanted to _____. You told me it was too tough carrying two mortgages. You told me you wanted to get down to your grandkids in Florida. Trust me. The same old thinking will yield the same old results. You want an expert? I'm that guy (or gal). I love your pink wallpaper, but unfortunately it doesn't matter what I think.

What matters is what buyers think, and according to market research it does make a difference. Mr. Seller, last year, high-end homes sold for X according to _____ or according to _____, and the year before they sold for Y. Why wouldn't you make a small investment of a half percent or one percent to get an additional six to eight percent according to data from the National Association of Realtors?"

NEXT LET'S DISCUSS THE THREE TYPES OF HOME STAGING

1. Vacant home: If the rooms are vacant, you will want to bring in furniture or digitally stage the space but it's always best to bring in actual furniture because people want to see how the room looks furnished. They want to sit in each room to get a feel for it. This will help create that emotional connection for the buyer. An empty home is hard to sell, so it is important to stage vacant spaces.

2. Accessorize a furnished home: Work with what the owners already have. Maybe just bring some light accessories in to refresh the space. Change things out, declutter, move artwork around to showcase it in the best place. Move furniture around to accentuate the best flow of the rooms and show the abundant space for families, entertaining, etc. Let's talk about location, location, location. Location is not just important in terms of where the home is located, but also where the placement of the furniture is within the room. The right placement is just as important as the type of furniture. Bring in some accent pieces as well. For example, maybe the owners have six dining room chairs that are prairie style, wood on wood, and you choose to remove two chairs to open up space. Another idea is to bring in some leather-bound chairs or some cloth bound to add interest and texture to the room. Accessorizing and other light staging is number two.

3. Complete staging: If you're working on an occupied home, you can

just hand over the keys to the stager. Let him or her just get to work. It's a clean slate. The stager might not move everything out, but they might move the living room furniture and make that the family room or vice versa. They might put items in storage, in the garage, or the basement, or have unnecessary items taken to one of those portable, on-demand storage units that can be moved to a new home. A stager might also bring in some of his or her inventory to help accessorize. Complete staging is the third type of staging.

THINGS TO CONSIDER ABOUT RETURN ON INVESTMENT AND STAGING

If a seller decides against staging their home, then they will have to reflect that with a discounted price because the majority of people can't see past their decorative taste. So, price aggressively and be ready to negotiate.

If they're not willing to reflect a discount in price, then they have to invest to have their home neutralized and have it staged. Home staging is just a "must do" task in the luxury market.

Let your clients know it could take years to sell a home that has not been staged. The high-end market is small compared to the rest of marketplace, and it could take a very long time to find a buyer that can purchase a luxury home, like their particular home, and can get past their personalized décor to see the potential for that house.

Sellers don't always hear this information with a willing ear, and they might disagree or refuse to listen to your advice. Overcoming objections is key to Sales 101. You are going to have to overcome objections on staging, and you're going to have to articulate this information better than your competition. You're going to have to be able to show them why they should stage their home and explain the benefits for them in the long

run. Remember to come back to this quote, "It doesn't matter what I think, Mr. Seller. What matters is what buyers think."

Let's talk about action steps next. Develop a relationship with a few stagers and add them to your vendor list. Also create your own "before" and "after" examples for various budgets, types, styles, and price points to help articulate the importance of staging to your clients.

You are going to want to have several "Before & After" case studies in your portfolio. Over the next several pages you see some examples for various styles and price points of homes. Included are examples for the following types of sellers: **Former sale by owner, Home staged by previous agent, Home that was too personalized, Vacant mansion, and a Virtually staged home.**

BEFORE AND AFTER
FOR SALE BY OWNER

851 Deer Path Court
Wheaton

Improvement Budget: $

Staging Budget: $

FOR SALE BY OWNER

Before

After

FOR SALE BY OWNER

Before

After

FOR SALE BY OWNER

FOR SALE BY OWNER

Before

After

FOR SALE BY OWNER

Before

After

Dominate Luxury Listings in Your Market

FOR SALE BY OWNER

Before

After

HOME STAGED BY PREVIOUS AGENT

1645 E Prairie Ave Wheaton

$1,395,000

Staging Budget: $3,000

Improvement Budget: $0

HOME STAGED BY PREVIOUS AGENT

Before

After

HOME STAGED BY PREVIOUS AGENT

HOME STAGED BY PREVIOUS AGENT

Before

After

HOME STAGED BY PREVIOUS AGENT

BEFORE AND AFTER NEUTRALIZATION & DECLUTTERING

13238 Wood Duck Drive
Plainfield

Improvement Budget: $

Staging Budget: $

NEUTRALIZATION & DECLUTTERING

Before

NEUTRALIZATION & DECLUTTERING

NEUTRALIZATION & DECLUTTERING

Before

After

NEUTRALIZATION & DECLUTTERING

Before

After

BEFORE AND AFTER VACANT MANSION

The Palace Royale

6501 S. County Line Road
Burr Ridge, IL

Improvement Budget: $ 0

VACANT MANSION

Before

After

VACANT MANSION

Before

After

VACANT MANSION

Before

After

VACANT MANSION

Before

After

VACANT MANSION

Before

After

VACANT MANSION

Before

After

BEFORE AND AFTER VIRTUAL STAGING

<u>999 N. Lake Shore Drive #9A</u>
<u>Chicago</u>

Improvement Budget: **$0**
Staging Budget: **$600**

VIRTUAL STAGING

Before

After

VIRTUAL STAGING

Before

After

VIRTUAL STAGING

VIRTUAL STAGING

Before

© VHT STUDIOS

After

VIRTUAL STAGING

> "It's imperative that you position the home most effectively so you accentuate the best features and downplay the least favorable.
>
> — Michael LaFido

LUXURY LISTING SPECIALIST PODCAST

CHAPTER 8 | 7 Best Practices to Utilizing Video to Sell Homes Faster

"If your dreams don't scare you, they are too small."

- Richard Branson

In this chapter, I'll be talking about best practices to utilize video to sell homes faster. I get a lot of brokerages and various companies asking me to present just on this chapter, so this is one of the most requested topics with information very relevant to your business. I will explain why the use of various type of videos is important, and I'm going to give plenty of video idea examples.

Why is video becoming more important in real estate? First, sellers want to use it, especially the higher end luxury sellers. In fact, 73 percent of sellers said they would hire an agent who uses video to market their home over an agent who doesn't use video. We are in a "show and tell" industry and video is becoming the latest way to achieve cutting-edge marketing of properties. If a picture is worth a thousand words, then I believe a video is worth a thousand pictures. Your video marketing is a way for you to easily differentiate yourself versus the competition in your industry, especially the dinosaurs or the traditional agents who are hesitant to utilize new technology. You can utilize videos on social media and send them in digital newsletters. Video is not optional anymore. It's the gold standard in visual marketing for high-end and luxury homes.

When creating videos, you need to leverage good thumbnails. A thumbnail is an image that is seen before someone clicks the play button to view your videos. The thumbnail needs to be enticing. YouTube will pick a thumbnail by default, but if you don't like the thumbnail they choose you will need to upload your own thumbnail.

BRIEFLY, LET'S GO OVER THE TOP SEVEN REASONS TO UTILIZE VIDEO

- Differentiation

- Builds trust

- Encourages social media shares

- Appeals to mobile users

- Google loves video

- Return on impression and a return on investment

- Boosts conversion

Apple's brilliant innovator Steve Jobs understood the power of video when he engineered "1984," which has been proclaimed as one of the most powerful TV commercials of all time. If you aren't familiar, "1984" is a legendary American television commercial that introduced the Apple Macintosh personal computer for the first time as part of the telecast of the third quarter of Super Bowl XVIII. It would be worth your time to find and view it online.

Now let's talk about what you need to get started making videos. I'm going to assume that if you don't use video already, you will need a video camera. You can buy a video camera or use your smartphone because the technology included with the latest models is pretty impressive and certainly sufficient for most real estate video purposes. Many of you might have a regular camera that you use to take pictures during the holidays or birthday parties. Many of those cameras also have video settings. Additionally, you can also use webcams. I recommend that you get a backdrop. A backdrop will be

helpful if you start to publish consistent educational videos from your office or home, and you will want to have a consistent background that looks professional. You also need a good microphone. I actually believe a microphone is a better, more important investment than a good camera. Is good sound more important than good video quality? I would say yes. Nobody will enjoy watching a video that sounds like you're in a wind tunnel. Good sound will add quality and professionalism to your videos.

What do you need next to get started? Create a YouTube account and then start to consistently post videos on your channel. To build a following, create different types of videos with content focused on many different topics. This variety will keep people interested in what you have to say. Additionally, create a nice, professional header image for your YouTube account.

WHAT ELSE CAN YOU DO WITH YOUR VIDEOS?
I have fifteen easy ways to use video to boost your business:

1. Post on social media channels and occasionally go "Live."

2. Post on your blog or your website.

3. Tour homes, open houses, or a coming-soon property.

4. Testimonials.

5. Feature your affiliates. Interview other people you work with. Ask them to share it on their social media, which will indirectly position you as the expert.

6. Use video at special events. Create lifestyle films, such as behind-the-scenes when you're creating a film.

7. Promotions like a contest or giveaway.

8. Case studies used for educational purposes.

9. Interviewing your clients for testimonials.

10. Educational videos on your blog or your social media.

11. Before and after pictures.

12. At your trainings.

13. In your emails and digital newsletters.

14. Advertise just-listed.

15. Showcase sold properties.

Video is all about strategic positioning, leveraging, and telling a story. If you could have every potential buyer's attention for two minutes, how would you use your time? Would you show still pictures like everyone else? Or would you present a luxurious video that better paints the picture of the lifestyle and benefits they could have in that luxury home? Do you see how much more effective this is than traditional means? Videos tap into the viewer's emotions. That is why I say a video is worth a thousand pictures. Another important point to remember is that real estate agents are limited to only a certain number of pictures on their local MLS, so that is one more reason video is an absolute necessity when selling a luxury home today.

For other lifestyle video ideas, my team has brought in props including: helicopters, vehicles, horses, actors, children, staging, trampolines, automobiles, artwork, and motorcycles. This is all part of proactive mar-

keting. We don't just list homes; we captivate buyers and buyers' agents by showcasing a lifestyle for them. We accentuate the best features of a home and its location not only through the pictures but especially through video.

Next, let's discuss action steps. Create your branded YouTube account and then start adding property videos and various types of real estate videos mentioned in this chapter. Remember, 73 percent of sellers said that they would hire a real estate agent that incorporated video rather than an agent that does not. Video is the new gold standard in visual marketing for luxury homes.

Video Is Not Optional

- Video Is The New Gold Standard In Visual Marketing Higher End & Luxury Homes
- Many Sellers Expect It

What You Need To Get Started

- Video Camera (phone/camera/webcam)
- Backdrop Is Optional
- Good Microphone
- Editing
- Topic
- Teleprompter
- Platform
- Visuals
- YouTube Channel

Bring Value With Content

Case Study On Website

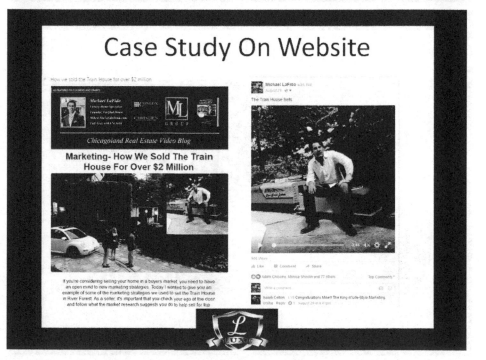

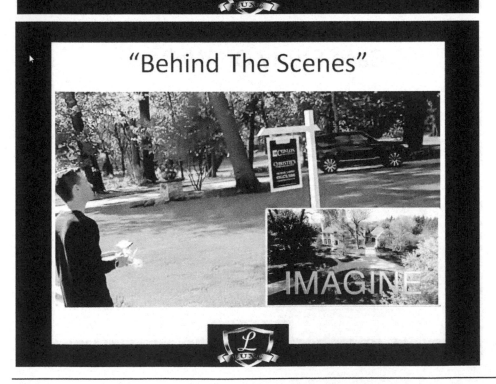

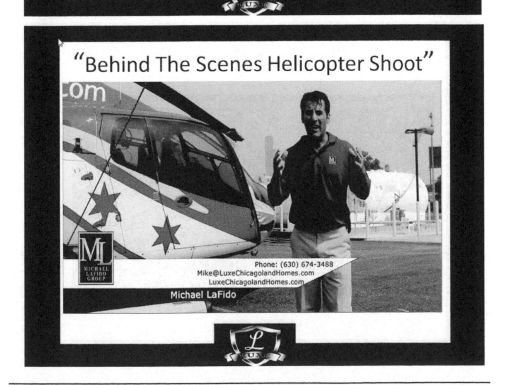

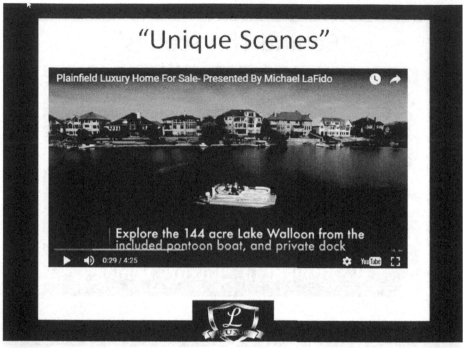

Lifestyle Films

FREE BONUS TRAINING

This bonus session includes **Step-by-step video training** on building a foundation to consistently sell luxury homes, the blueprint to attract luxury sellers, and how to use video to position yourself as a luxury authority in your market.

Get it **NOW** at LuxuryListingBlueprint.com

" The magic happens when people step out of their comfort zone. "

- Michael LaFido

LUXURY LISTING SPECIALIST PODCAST

CHAPTER 9 | The Steve Jobs Approach to Selling Luxury Homes

*"You're not in the real estate business.
You're in the business of marketing your real
estate business."*
- Michael LaFido

Let's talk a little more about Apple's Steve Jobs. He wasn't just an innovator, and he didn't just sell Apple products. He was a marketing genius. He perfected the product launch, artistically painted pictures in the minds of his customers by selling features and their benefits, and he captured the emotions of his audience. Jobs was a revolutionary thinker; he was a visionary. If you have read any of Steve Jobs' quotes, then you know he was anything but traditional. Many of my business models, including my consulting business, stem from his words:

"Here's to the crazy ones, the rebels, the misfits, the ones who see things differently. They may have no respect for the status quo. You can disagree with them, glorify, or vilify them, but about the only thing you can't do is ignore them. They push the human race forward. And while some may see them as the crazy ones, we see genius. Because the people who are crazy enough to think they can change the world, are the ones who do."

– Steve Jobs, *Apple*

Steve Jobs also perfected leveraging. Let's get into some specifics. In this age of social media, it is very important to have validity and social proof. In the early 2000s many consumers thought if they read something on the Internet it had to be true. The exact opposite of that is true today; most consumers browsing the Internet are skeptical by nature. That is why review sites like Angie's List and Yelp, or even Zillow reviews of real

estate agents are more and more popular. Third-party validation is very important. Why am I sharing this with you? When marketing a home, most agents tell a potential buyer how unique the property or estate is, or what a great deal it is, or how they can't rebuild this home at the same cost. It is an entirely different approach, and much more authentic, to capture the home on video and sell the lifestyle to bring out the emotions of the buyer.

These days people are skeptical by nature, so any press coverage and positive exposure for a home is helpful. Steve Jobs had a huge platform to help him at Apple. **What if there was a way to create massive exposure and buzz with local and national media outlets for your listing?** How about getting local business owners, key influencers, and the media talking about that home? Do you think having celebrities talking about your listing would be helpful when selling? Would that be more effective than utilizing traditional marketing alone? Of course it would. I'm going to share those Steve Jobs leveraging methods with you. Leverage the power of video, professional pictures, and event-based marketing to sell the lifestyle. It is not an option in today's luxury real estate marketplace. It's a necessity.

START BY TELLING STORIES

Marketing a luxury home is different than marketing other types of properties. **Market research has concluded the most effective means of marketing luxury homes is by selling a lifestyle to the potential buyer.** It's nearly impossible to do that without the use of professional video. I touched on this already, but stories sell and touch peoples' emotions. This is a skill that Steve Jobs mastered. Think about the most influential leaders today. They are great at storytelling. Like him or not, former President Barack Obama was a great storyteller, and he captivated the audience when he spoke (at least when his teleprompter worked).

Think of most of the popular churches today. The pastors don't just read from the Bible, they tell stories so their audience can follow along and stay engaged, bringing out emotions and keeping the audience's attention. Some of my best ideas and marketing pieces didn't come from the real estate industry. If storytelling is good enough for Steve Jobs and Apple, then why wouldn't it be a good idea to use that approach to sell luxury homes?

Steve Jobs and Apple surveyed and conducted research on their clients before going to market with a new product. Information gathering is not optional. Whether I'm marketing a luxury home as a Realtor, consulting with a homeowner directly, or coaching another Realtor, we conduct extensive research. We interview others to gather as much information as we can about the location, area attractions, and history of the home to showcase its uniqueness. We want to understand the owners' reasons for falling in love with their home and its location. We start by asking the homeowner for the top ten reasons they originally purchased the home as well as the details of the property. We also interview the architect and the builder. With this information, a detailed special feature sheet can be created to best illustrate the benefits and lifestyle accompanying that particular luxury home. However, these special feature sheets are only effective when a buyer or a buyer's agent inquires or physically views the home. This tool is supplemented with exceptional photos and amazing videos of the home. Finally, massive exposure is created through our proprietary systems to get buyers and media outlets to visit the home property's website to receive more information on the home and view the professional video. We do this to help potential buyers, but we also do this to make the agent's job easier when showing one of the properties we represent.

Next, let's discuss the "product launch," which in the real estate world means going "live" on the MLS. Many congruencies exist between a

product launch and a "property launch." Everything leading up to the home going live on the MLS can be compared to the preparation of a product launch. From the time you get the signed listing agreement to all the preparation involved in getting a home prepared for the professional photos, launching a property on the MLS could be compared to a product launch. We look at the positioning of the home for the first time on the MLS as a product launch. When Steve Jobs and Apple launched products like the iPad, or previously the iPod, they created buzz surrounding the product. This buzz would heighten consumers' and media outlets' interest. Anticipation then rose to a fever pitch, resulting in sellouts in many stores. Those lengthy lines with people waiting to buy these new products were all due to buzz and demand fostered prior to the product launch. So how do you create a buzz and excitement around a property when you are in a buyer's market and there are years of inventory? After studying Steve Jobs, I have applied the same approach to creating a buzz for buyers, brokers, and media outlets at the local, national, and international levels. **More exposure and more press will lead to more showings, which ultimately leads to more offers!**

Do you see the calculated difference between just "listing" a home on the MLS (like most "traditional" agents do) versus "marketing" a home with the product launch approach? I hope you are starting to understand how strategies shared in this chapter "The Steve Jobs Approach to Selling Luxury Homes" would be helpful in marketing a luxury home today. Luxury homes have a drastically higher chance at selling with this approach, so I encourage you to try these techniques on your next listing.

How about specific action steps? You will need to "craft the story" for the property that you are marketing. Remember to highlight the best features of the home and the location in all of your marketing efforts and property launch.

The Steve Jobs Approach To Selling Luxury Homes

- Leverage
- Steve Jobs Sold Telling Stories
- Research
- Product Launch (Media)
- Videos Are Engaging
- Event Based Marketing
- Highlight The Kitchen

Tell The "Story" Of The Home In Writing Along With The Special Features

Coming Soon

Lifestyle Films

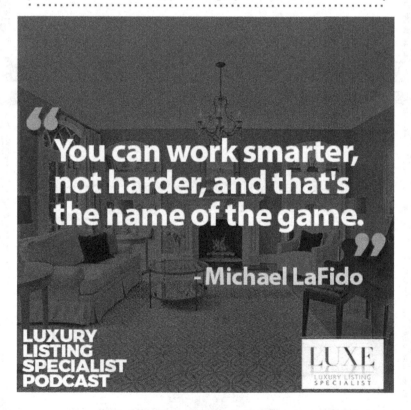

CHAPTER 10 | Why Lifestyle Marketing Is Not Optional Anymore

"People often say that motivation doesn't last. Well, neither does bathing–that's why we recommend it daily."

- Zig Ziglar

Let's get right into the ideas behind "lifestyle" marketing. This chapter is going to contain a lot of visuals because they illustrate the effectiveness of these ideas better than explanations. A lifestyle is a brand, a company that embodies interests, attitudes, and opinions of a certain group or culture. In this case the potential buyers are the group or culture. Lifestyle brands seek to inspire, guide, and motivate with a goal of their products being purchased to contribute to the definition of the customer's or consumer's way of life.

For example, this is the lifestyle marketing message you want to send to potential buyers for your listing: If you buy this home, your life is going to be great because of A, B, C, and D. You can forget about the rat race when you get home at night, and you will enjoy A, B, C, D for work, play, and everything in between. What we're trying to do is accentuate the best features of the home and the location while downplaying the least favorable. It's our job as the agent to create and circulate that message for the property.

Next, let's talk a little bit about storytelling. Storytelling in real estate involves describing the home through the MLS description, in the narrative, the agent remarks that real estate agents see, the pictures, or the story within a video that you create. Perhaps it's also the story you tell in the brochures or the special features. Typical copywriting describes home features like breathtaking views, abundant closet storage, and great en-

tertaining space. Lifestyle writing focuses on how living in the home and its location can lead to a happier, healthy, and more meaningful life for the buyer and their family for generations to come.

Tell the story of the house in your property features. For some of our high-end properties, we have anywhere from five-to ten-page special feature sheets where the opening paragraph is the narrative of the house that leads through room by room, telling a story about each of the rooms. Many agents just plainly state "Front foyer, 13X10, hardwood floors; living room, 20X16, scraped walnut floors." No, that will not cut it just describing the dimensions in written format for each of the areas. Try describing the kitchen like this, "Enjoy the gourmet kitchen for cooking holiday meals and casual carry-out spread across the island. Dishes won't feel like as much work with a picture window above the sink overlooking the tree-lined backyard and pond." Think along the lines of how potential buyers will actually want to use these spaces, and paint a picture of an ideal lifestyle for them in that house. You can also tell the story of the home with pictures, videos, descriptions, and marketing materials. Sometimes a picture alone will tell a story without any words or video.

There are a few things to remember with lifestyle video production. Check on the regulations and guidelines within your MLS regarding video usage. In many Realtor associations, there are still rules regarding video details, such as having people in virtual tours, so be sure you study what you can and cannot do before investing your time and money.

Let's continue talking about videos, though, specifically telling a story with video. Videos must be engaging, and they can't be too long. They can't be shot too fast and have a shaky picture because it looks unprofessional, and quite frankly, difficult to watch. It's all about strategic positioning, leveraging, and telling a story. Today, only 2 percent of real estate agents consistently utilize lifestyle videos to market homes, and

only 12 percent of real estate agents have an active YouTube account where they're updating videos regularly. Recently I sold a home that is located in a buyer's market. We had an offer price at 97 percent of the asking price. In this particular community, homes are selling for around 90 percent of the asking price. I asked the buyer's agent, "Hey, did your clients see the video?" She said, "You mean the YouTube video?" I said, "Yeah." Then she said, "My client did not want to live in this town anymore. They live here. They wanted to get out of here because of high taxes and poor schools. They saw your video. He contacted me. He said, 'we need to go see this home.'" After they saw the home, boom, he in put an offer. The video I created and posted allowed those buyers to imagine themselves in that home, just like when we discussed the effectiveness of staging. Buyers have to be able to visualize themselves living in the home. You want them to imagine themselves being happy and comfortable in that space.

When you create a great video, you need to have amazing thumbnails that are calling people to click on it. Those great thumbnails need to make people say, "Wow. I want to click on this. This looks amazing." When you have these videos to use for promotion, you want to leverage them. You want to get photos. You want to get views. You want that video to go viral, and of course you want people talking about the home and even your strategies. You want people saying, "This guy is aggressive. He's outside the box."

You can leverage your videos through the press, through the media, and through your luxury networking group. They're going to know that you're different, and you can offer services that other agents cannot. They're going to want to refer business to you because you're different. You will definitely want to leverage your videos on a website platform where prospective clients visit your site and click through your videos. Your potential clients will be even more pre-sold on you once they receive your rock star

package or your shock-and-awe package (AKA pre-listing package). The goal is for them to say, "Wow, nobody else is doing this kind of stuff."

Next, how can you leverage a lifestyle film or a lifestyle event? You can do a Facebook Live video while shooting the lifestyle film, or you can do a case study Facebook Live video. An effective idea might be to do a video on a home that recently sold, and start it, "One of the things that we did to get this property sold," and then talk about how your methods are different and grab attention from prospective buyers. Just do a short, two-to three-minute video, and you'll get some great response–social proof that your strategies work.

When you have great videos, photos, and great marketing, you want to leverage it. Get your affiliates talking about the work you're doing, and also get your networking group talking about it. Additionally, get your office to start talking about it, and even local media. You want to boost any videos you created through Facebook and Facebook Live. Let's conclude this chapter by talking about action steps. Film your first lifestyle video and promote the heck out it. Utilize Facebook Live videos in ways to help build your brand.

Telling The "Story" With Pictures

Backs to the Chicago Golf Club

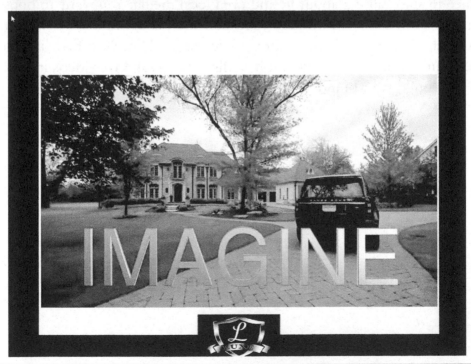

IMAGINE

Lifestyle Marketing

Best Features

Dominate Luxury Listings in Your Market

River Forest Express

Twister Themed Bathroom

> " We are blessed to have the responsibility to help people. "
>
> - Michael LaFido

LUXURY LISTING SPECIALIST PODCAST

CHAPTER 11 | How to Leverage Event-Based Marketing to Attract Buyers and More Clients

"Success leaves clues. Surround yourself with good people that are hungrier than you are."
- Tony Robbins

Event-based marketing is an effective way to sell your luxury listing. My team has had abundant success with our properties by creating massive exposure both online and offline by getting the right people to talk about the home to potential buyers.

This is similar to the product launch strategy that we discussed in chapter 9. Event-based marketing involves hosting an event around a specific cause with key community members and celebrities. We are not talking about the boring, traditional open house with non-producing brokers that show up for the free wine and cheese. I'm talking about an event—an exclusive event. Those in attendance would be potential buyers, business owners, celebrities, local media outlets and the press, or others that are influential in the high-net-worth individuals sphere of influence. Other attendees would be sponsors that include luxury car dealers, high-end art dealers, and business owners. There would be a press release and a video crew present to create massive exposure and buzz in the community and on social media. Additionally, a security company, high-end magazines, home theater builders, attorneys, and CPAs would be invited. This is your target audience, so you want to cover all the bases in terms of their lifestyle and showcase that the home fits in with everything else they want and need to continue thriving professionally and personally.

Those are the basics of event-based marketing. This is going to be an exciting chapter for you. Again, we're working to build social proof for

our business, and we're talking about high-net-worth individuals and influencers in that community. So let's talk about hosting a luxury event. Who's on your list? Who gets the invite? How do you put together a list of your top high-net-worth individuals and influencers?

The luxury event is something for which I have seen a great return on impression and return on investment. I recommend trying it at one of your high-end properties or luxury homes, versus a neutral location. It could be a property that's not on the market with you. Maybe you know somebody that owns a mansion or a beautiful home, and they're willing to host it because they like networking and perhaps showing off a little. There are a lot of things to consider when hosting a luxury event, including safety, security of the property, insurance, and liability. Again, check with your broker, check with the homeowner, check with your insurance provider who does the insurance of your business, or even your own home. It's as simple as making a call saying, "Hey, I'm looking at hosting an event. I want to make sure I'm completely protected should someone get hurt, slip and fall, or something happens to the home, etc." This is very important. You might even hire an event planner if you want a bit more assistance.

Be careful about who you entrust with helping run the event if you decide to hire additional help. Recently I had an event where I made the event planner put down a deposit. She told me, "Oh yeah, we clean up, we'll get the garbage removed and put everything back just like it was before, etc." I said, "Well, put this money down and I'll release it should you do what you say you're going to do, but I don't want to have to go back over to the home and clean up. I want the home better and cleaner after the event than it was before."

You have to be skeptical, and you have to cover yourself with contracts, and even have attorneys look things over, because if something unfortunate happens to the home or someone at the home, we do not want to

be held financially or legally responsible. We have to protect ourselves, our families, and our business. We've all heard stories about people going to the properties for the wrong reasons, whether they are looking to steal something, or they're faking an injury because it's a rain storm and they slipped and fell. Protect yourself, and always error on the side of caution. Next let's move on to sponsorship for the event. Sponsors are always a good option to consider because they help alleviate the cost. You might even break even after an event, but more importantly, you're asking the sponsors to invite their top influencers. The power is in the invite. You want high-net-worth individuals and high-net-worth influencers in that community to be telling people about the event and sharing it on their social media. You have to define what your expectation is of your sponsors, and you have to hold them to it. Communication is key to a successful working relationship and future sponsorships.

Here is an example of how powerful an invite can be. Maybe you are married, and let's say you invited 300 people to your wedding, and you know going into it 20 percent won't be able to attend. That's pretty typical. You might get 240 people at your reception. Now, with a luxury event like this, you're going to get a lot less than 50 percent of people showing up. Require an RSVP because you need a head count for the caterers and security. Usually, about 25-50 percent of the people we invite actually attend, and 50 percent is on the high end. It's really about 25-35 percent who attend. However, people talk about the event, and they appreciate being invited to such an exclusive, well-publicized gathering. The power is ultimately in the invite.

With successful events, you're building your brand, and a return on impression. Return on impressions are for those two-thirds of people that aren't going to come. You're positioning yourself in the community and industry. You're building trust, and you're building credibility by having these types of events. Look at the power of association with Bentley, Jag-

uar, Mercedes-Benz, Steinway & Sons, and Lamborghini. There's power of association with products just like with an event.

At the event itself, you've got to have some structure. I recommend a check-in for guests, give them a goodie bag when they leave, give guided tours of the home, and have security at the property. You can (and should) invite the press to the event. It's important to invite all the big influencers in the local media for event-based marketing. When my team did an event with Ferrari, we had people showing up, taking photos, doing Facebook Lives, doing test drives. That is a perfect opportunity for some great media coverage.

In addition to community members, neighbors, art dealerships, car dealers, and high-end clothing boutiques, you can invite local nonprofits. You can tie in a nonprofit by donating proceeds from the event to a certain cause, or you might have multiple charities in attendance. They can bring in tables and have informational booths, working to make some connections with potential donors or board members. Logistically, use video announcements and nice, high-end marketing materials in the goodie bags and for the invite. Above all else, cover yourself liability-wise. Protect yourself.

Let's go over a few more details about offering goodie bags to guests. At our events, we always give a goodie bag to guests when they leave. All of the sponsors put something of value in the goodie bag, which makes a great statement and also promotes the sponsors' business. We put brochures in the goodie bag about the property and information about why they should hire us if they're in the market to sell. Of course, my business card is always in there too. Use the goodie bag as a way to promote your business as well as the home.

Remember, the experience of coming to the event is important for high-

net-worth individuals. If the overall experience of an event is great for your guests, you're going to get referrals from it, guaranteed. After an event I did with Ferrari, I had a $2 million listing appointment the next day with someone who attended the event. Even if you have a high-net-worth luxury client, and they don't want to attend this event because they're really private, there's a perceived value in the invite. That client might think, "Man, this guy's a mover and a shaker, and he's got a powerful network." This could certainly lead to some business opportunities.

One really important factor you need to keep in mind is know your buyer. We promoted an event at a home that I previously had under contract for over $2.5 million. It has a Twister-themed bathroom and the home is near Wrigley Field. These former clients of mine are from the LGBT community and they wanted to team up with a cruise line that caters to that community. In this particular area of Chicago, there are a lot of people from the LGBT community, so we teamed up with the cruise line that caters to that community and did a cocktails and appetizer event at the property. We promoted the event, we promoted the home, we promoted the brochure, and we promoted the agents who cater to that community. Knowing your buyer is one more way to differentiate yourself as an agent.

Another event idea that my team has done is a client appreciation party at a high-end property that I was selling around the holidays. We teamed up with an event planner and had nonprofits there, and we held a "get your photo with Santa" opportunity. We also featured different tasting stations, wine stations, and much more. That was a really fun, festive way to get prospective buyers and influencers into a home.

We always hope that this event directly sells the home, but indirectly we're letting people know about the listing and our business in a creative, outside-the-box way. Other sellers in the area, other luxury home owners in the area, and other valuable contacts will talk about the event, which could lead to promising future prospects.

Let's talk about action steps. Host an event at one of your higher end listings or at an upscale location in the next 90 to 180 days. Remember that the power is in the invite.

Event-Based Marketing

Who's On The List?

"The Power Is In The Invite"

- Influencers (luxury networking group, press, business owners, community, neighbors)
- Art Dealer/Car Dealer/Clothing/High End/Nonprofit Tie In/Celebrities
- Valet, Catered Food, Music, etc.

Your Network Is Your Net Worth

Test Drive: Red, White, Or Blue

Luxury Event

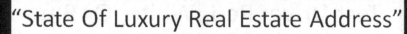

"State Of Luxury Real Estate Address"

Art OF SPEED

DYNAMIC EXPERIENCE *INVITATION*

Together with Ferrari North America, CONLON/Christie's International Real Estate invites you to experience the elegance, sportiness, versatility and breathtaking performance of the Ferrari California T at the Ferrari Art of Speed driving experience.

THE PERFECT SYNTHESIS OF INNOVATION AND TECHNOLOGY

The Ferrari California T's new twin-turbo V8 is a classic Ferrari engine, reinvented for a new generation, delivering instantaneous throttle response, blistering performance, impressive torque and a signature soundtrack.

THURSDAY, JUNE 2ND, 2016
3:00 PM – 7:00 PM

PRIVATE WHEATON ESTATE
Call or text Michael LaFido at 630-674-3488 to RSVP

RSVP

To schedule your personal driving experience or for more information, please contact us at CaliforniaT@ferrariartofspeed.com or call 201-706-7007.

Please note that all drivers must be at least 25 years of age, possess a valid driver's license and automobile insurance.

Dominate Luxury Listings in Your Market

.... YOU ARE INVITED TO OUR ....

Client Appreciation Party

A party to say Thank You to those who have supported us!

Hosted by Michael LaFido

DECEMBER 15
6:00 – 9:00pm

*Culinary taste sensations, fine wines,
carolers & much more*

Please RSVP by Monday, December 12
Mike@TheLaFidoTeam.com
(Details provided upon RSVP)

The Palace Royale, 6501 S.County Line Rd, Burr Ridge

This home is currently listed for sale for $10,950,000. For more pictures and details, please visit ThePalaceRoyale.com

"People don't care how much you know, until they know you care."

— Michael LaFido

LUXURY LISTING SPECIALIST PODCAST

CHAPTER 12 | How to Utilize Publicity and Media to Sell More Listings

"All wealthy top achievers have coaches."

- James Malinchak

In this chapter, we're going to be talking about the differences between advertising and public relations, and also how you build relationships with the media.

There are benefits with PR versus advertising. Advertising is paid, versus PR, which is earned. Advertising builds exposure, while PR builds trust. In real estate, great PR is invaluable because high-net-worth individuals, luxury clients, and higher end contacts all need to build considerable trust in you and your business. Advertisements are simply commercials, and are often flipped through and forgotten. A great public relations piece tells a story and is more believable. Advertising, however, does directly create brand, but PR is a third-party branding, which is even more powerful. The best route for your business is totally up to you and your goals. How do you want to brand yourself? Another point to consider is that ads are mostly visual while PR uses more language and tells stories.

Be cautious about what information is given to the media. Local beat writers, reporters, and national news writers tend to care about what's in it for them. They have a job to do. If you can hand them a story, something that's unique, controversial, different, outside the box, and cutting edge, then they'll return your call. They care about publishing an interesting, engaging story that will keep their news outlet at the forefront. They will not put "boring" news in print or online, and especially not on TV, so be careful to only submit media releases when you know you've

got something special to share.

There has been a significant shift in coverage when it comes to luxury real estate. Top press outlets with a heavy online presence are now narrowing their scope of coverage to generate more hits and traction on their sites. Today, the bigger the "wow" factor or celebrity intrigue of a home, the better.

There are a lot of opportunities at the local media level, which can help promote and brand your business. These opportunities will eventually open doors to the larger media outlets, which will then open doors at the national level. You've got to start small and work on gaining momentum. It's a compound effect. Little successes with local media or one of the local small papers in your market will help you build credibility.

When dealing with the media, you need to own the numbers. That's one way you can establish yourself as an expert in this business. You need to understand the current trends locally, nationally, and worldwide. Specifically, you need to be able to articulate those numbers and trends to your database, to your sphere of influence, and especially to the media. It would be a great idea to develop regular reports or educational videos to keep all of these contacts in the loop.

When making contact with the media. I would send them your "rock star" pre-listing package with other press that you've received, the other properties you've sold, or an invite to an event, and your book or website link (whatever is applicable). Do some social media scouting to find common ground with impotent media contacts. Maybe you share some similar connections, and somebody could make a powerful introduction. That's the best way to make an impression instead of just cold calling them.

Here's an example of an effective way to leverage your contacts for new introductions:

John Thorne is friends with Ron Muhitch. Ron a great reporter for the *Wall Street Journal*. If you're friends with John, ask him to make that introduction. "Hey, John Thorne. I see that you're connected with Ron Muhitch. Would you mind making an introduction for me? I would really appreciate it. As a matter of fact, I actually wrote a sample introduction for you. You can use all of it, or you can use none of it, but I thought I would at least help you because your time is valuable." Many times, your friend will copy and paste it and send that introduction. That is a great action for you because you get to control that first impression. Now when you follow up with Ron Muhitch, he'll maybe return your call, or at least you can name drop Thorne because you know that first introduction has been made. That's going to be really important in building your business and press coverage.

CASE STUDY:
HOW I RECEIVED MY FIRST MAJOR PRESS COVERAGE
"Will a $10,000 movie with actors, Bentleys, and horses sell this home?"

I should start by noting that I was working to get press coverage for an upcoming lifestyle video. I Googled a member of the press and I realized that he does most of the real estate stories in the area. I just Googled his name and got his number. I was prepared with my remarks in case he picked up. He did pick up. Ring, ring. "Dennis Rodkin."

"Hey, Dennis, this is Michael LaFido. You don't know who I am."

At the time, I was with the Sotheby's brand. I said, "I'm with Sotheby's. Hey, I have an amazing property I'm putting on the market. I'm not sure if you're interested in a story that you've probably never run with, that's totally outside-the-box unconventional, that will grab people's attention. If so, then I have something for you. If not, that's okay."

Of course, he said, "Well, you've piqued my curiosity. What have you got?"

I said, "Well, I'm going to be shooting a lifestyle film in a few days at a $4.5 million property. I'm going to have two film crews there. I'm bringing in actors, horses, Bentleys, Lamborghinis. We're going to have drones there. It's going to be amazing. It's about a $10,000 film for me to do."

He says, "Wow, that's amazing. Let me check with my editor and I'll call you back." Within five minutes he called me and said, "We're going to go with it." The next day, he called me back for an interview, and the day after that this was the lead story on ChicagoBusiness.com. I couldn't have asked for better coverage. My phone was ringing off the hook.

To make this story even better, ABC called me. They were going to send a film crew out that next day. We shot the lifestyle film on a Monday morning. I'll never forget it. I was so stressed out because my film crews were calling me on Sunday saying, "Hey, there's an 80 percent chance of rain tomorrow."

All I could say was, "I've got way too many moving parts. I've got four luxury cars being transported here. I've got a horse. I've got actors." I said, "I need you guys to be there rain or shine. If we can't film, we can't film, but we're not calling it off." Well, of course, that was going to cost me money if they had to sit on-site and not film. However, we rolled the dice, and the good Lord was on my side that day. It didn't rain, and we got some amazing PR out of that shoot. How did I get the PR? I picked up the phone. It was just a cold call, but I was prepared and knew what I was going to say. I knew it was a unique story that people would be interested in. That's going to be really important to remember as you work to increase press coverage. What would you want to read about, listen to, or watch? Bring value to the media. Understand what people are

interested in. Remember, press members are looking for stories that are controversial, cutting edge, or totally new and outside the box. Just like I said push the edge and let them know about the amazing things you're doing with your business. That's what they're looking for. The traditional cookie-cutter route just won't work for real estate stories unless there is a celebrity attached to the home or it has historic value. Those stories tend to garner enough interest just based on their universal appeal.

Let's go over specific action steps. Start developing relationships with local media outlets. When you or your properties are featured in various publications, make sure that you leverage the articles to your database and on your social media accounts to ensure it reaches as many people as possible.

Thursday, August 7th, 2014 | This Week's Crain's

ChicagoBusiness.com

CRAIN'S
CHICAGO BUSINESS.

Who's hiring
This list | New h

Trending | Crate & Barrel • Red Line work • Trib sto

News | Blogs | Multimedia | Lists | Small Bu

STANDARD BANK AND TRUST CO.
Member FDIC

Will a $10,000 movie with actors, Bentleys and horses sell this home?

A real estate agent is shooting a movie at a Barrington Hills estate that evokes memories of "Lifestyles of the Rich and Famous," wagering it will help him sell the seven-acre

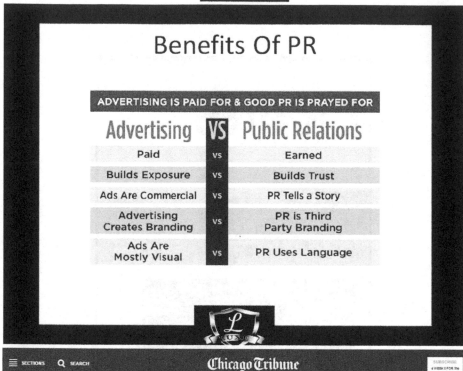

f   y   ✉   Classified / Real Es

Trains, Trump or a Twister shower — It'll cost you $3 million

In case you missed it

 Contemporary home in Logan Square: $1.09M
APR. 15, 2016

Corner penthouse in River North: $1.249M
APR. 13, 2016

A $3 million, 7700-square-foot River Forest home for sale along Ashland Avenue. (James C. Svehla/Chicago Tribune)

By **Susan Moskop**
Chicago Tribune

APRIL 21, 2016

> "**Give them confidence that you're the right person to be talking with.**"
>
> — **Michael LaFido**

LUXURY LISTING SPECIALIST PODCAST

Summary, Implementation & Action Steps

As you finish this book, my goal was to motivate and inspire you to take action to sell more high-end and luxury homes in the next year. It is possible when you implement the action steps I've outlined in each chapter and use the information you've learned throughout these chapters.

I know that it is not easy to stay motivated to build and grow your real estate business profitably while maintaining your sanity, health, marriage, relationship with your kids, work/life balance, and having a happy and sound spiritual life.

But it's entirely possible to take a few shortcuts that can and will get you results and earn more money faster without spending all the time and effort it normally takes to break into or dominate selling luxury homes.

If you've enjoyed and learned from what you've read (or most of what you've read), I would absolutely love to hear from you and get to know you better. I would also appreciate you posting a success story, picture, or video, and comment at: www.facebook.com/groups/luxurylisting.

It is my pleasure to help you learn to successfully sell homes in the higher-end and luxury price points.

Prove Them Wrong!

Michael LaFido

Michael LaFido
Founder & CEO
O: 888.930.8510 |
E: Michael@MarketingLuxuryGroup.com

To help agents demonstrate their skills, I have created a luxury broker certification. This new designation establishes a minimum set of standards for agents. My program instills the same principles I outline in my book, "Marketing Luxury," and teach through my Marketing Luxury Group.

It offers potential clients third-party validation through documented, hands-on training and certification. Most agents spend years trying to secure luxury listings; many never get them. With this certification, agents have access to proven and repeatable marketing systems, which can be utilized in the marketing of their luxury listings. This certification and the training agents receive as part of this program will almost single-handedly pull the luxury real estate niche out of the Dinasauric Age. Agents are seeing astounding results from these pioneering methods.

To learn more on how to get certified, please visit
LUXURYLISTINGSPECIALIST.COM.

ONLINE ACCESS TO ALL TRAINING AND MATERIALS

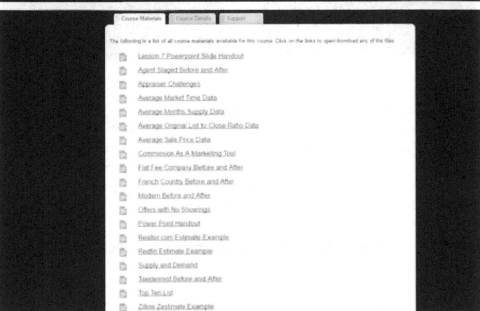

To learn more on how to get certified, please visit
LUXURYLISTINGSPECIALIST.COM

Want to break into selling high end homes? Subscribe to the Luxury Listing Specialist Podcast

MANAGEMENT & MARKETING

Where top luxury agents reveal their best practices PLUS interviews with real estate industry influencers, thought leaders and luxury marketing experts, you'll come away from each episode with new strategies and tactics to list and sell high-end homes in ANY market.

www.LuxuryListingPodcast.com

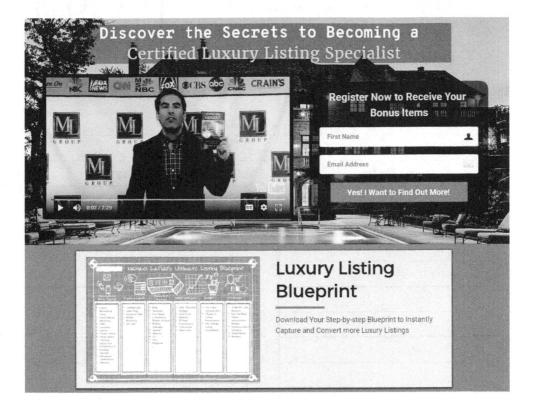

This bonus session includes Step-by-step video training on building a foundation to consistently sell luxury homes, the blueprint to attract luxury sellers, and how to use video to position yourself as a luxury authority in your market.

Get it NOW at
LUXURYLISTINGBLUEPRINT.COM

Luxury Listing Specialist

The "AH-HA" Action Planner

90-Day Plan To Turn Your "AH-HA" Ideas Into Action

Top 3 Goals		

30 Days

60 Days

90 Days

Future Project "Parking Lot"